FIRST EDITION

A TUTORING PRIMER:

READING WITH K-6 STRUGGLING READERS, ENGLISH LEARNERS, AND FAMILIES

By Julie L. Pennington and Rachel G. Salas

cognella® | ACADEMIC PUBLISHING

Bassim Hamadeh, CEO and Publisher

Kassie Graves, Director of Acquisitions and Sales

Jamie Giganti, Senior Managing Editor

Miguel Macias, Senior Graphic Designer

Alisa Munoz, Licensing Coordinator

Abbey Hastings, Associate Production Editor

Cover image copyright © 2016 by iStockphoto LP/gradyreese.

copyright © 2013 by iStockphoto LP/kali9.

copyright © 2016 by iStockphoto LP/asiseeit.

copyright © 2016 by iStockphoto LP/vgajic.

copyright © 2016 by iStockphoto LP/Steve Debenport.

copyright © 2016 by iStockphoto LP/Weekend Images Inc.

copyright © 2014 by iStockphoto LP/kali9.

copyright © 2016 by iStockphoto LP/kali9.

copyright © 2013 by iStockphoto LP/fstop123.

Printed in the United States of America

ISBN: 978-1-5165-0798-6 (pbk) / 978-1-5165-0799-3 (br) / 978-1-5165-4628-2 (al)

CONTENTS

PREFACE

We have taught struggling readers through university courses and programs for over a decade. We both now teach a university-based tutoring clinic for struggling readers. The clinic tutoring is designed to teach future teachers how to assess and instruct young readers in grades K-6. We also work with an outreach tutoring grant that puts university students in schools to tutor struggling readers. Both tutoring programs focus on making sure struggling readers enjoy reading and writing as they make progress. We believe all children are readers and writers, and we strive to collaborate with families and base our work on the interests and strengths of the children. Both of us bring our experiences and knowledge into the program, and now to this text.

Julie Pennington taught for 14 years in a bilingual dual-language school, initially as a first-grade teacher of English learners, then finally as a fifth/sixth-grade teacher. Her last five years of teaching took her out of the classroom as she became a Reading Recovery teacher and taught struggling first graders one-on-one within Marie Clay's program. She also taught struggling second- and third-graders in small intervention groups. Julie has been a teacher-educator for 14 years and directed the university reading clinic for the past five years. She and Rachel worked together at graduate school in 2000 and now both work in the reading clinic.

Rachel Salas has taught upper elementary grades in urban schools in East Los Angeles and southeast Washington, DC. She taught fourth and sixth grade and spent several years as a fourth/fifth grade multiage bilingual teacher. She has spent 16 years as a teacher educator at universities across the nation. As a teacher-educator, she has taught reading diagnosis and been involved with a university on-campus and in-school tutoring program for over 14 years.

ACKNOWLEDGMENTS

We thank our graduate assistants, Hannah Carter and Erica Charles, for all of their assistance with the book, and our university tutors, Sally, Marisa, Emma, Anastasia, Jonathon, Kit, Emily, Ashley, Raina, Hulsey, Crystal, Lindsey, and Carli. We also express our gratitude to the families for bringing their children to us twice a week for 11 weeks and allowing our students to grow and develop as educators. Finally, thank you to our families for all their love and support throughout the writing process.

INTRODUCTION

Our purpose is to bring tutoring support to a broad audience of tutors—those of you in courses learning to teach, others working in programs within schools, or volunteers looking for ways to become more effective tutors. While there are many tutoring textbooks that are very detailed and reflect the complex nature of reading and writing instruction, they do not necessarily begin at a place for novice tutors. We wanted to create a textbook for tutors in teacher education programs who have little to no knowledge of reading and writing instruction, and present the information in a way they can access and understand quickly as they begin to tutor. This book provides foundational knowledge of content, pedagogy, and assessment in an accessible format with accompanying videos. Theory is mentioned and supporting research is cited. The videos depict both specific instructional methods and also case studies of students. The main difference between our title and other tutoring books is the word **primer**, as defined by Merriam-Webster:

Definition of PRIMER

1. a small book for teaching children to read

2. a small introductory book on a subject

3. a short informative piece of writing

Primers are specifically used in elementary instruction as the first books students use when they are learning to read in school. This book is best used as the first book tutors read before they move to the more advanced and sophisticated tutoring books designed for advanced courses.

The book is organized into five sections and can be read out of order, since each section stands alone. We begin with definitions of "literacy" before discussing how language and literacy are acquired by young children. The second part of the text highlights the basic areas of reading and writing, and how to teach and assess each area. The third section is focused on how to specifically teach reading and writing and includes lesson plans and ideas for adapting instruction to your own needs. Lesson plans are set up for beginning, intermediate, and advanced tutors. The final section covers communicating with families and how to adapt instruction for individual student needs through case study examples. We utilize accompanying videos to assist you with clear examples of instruction and assessment.

As you read...

When you see this Active Learning icon:

Go to your online Active Learning portal.

PART I: WHAT IS LITERACY?

Literacy is a common term and used often, yet what does it mean to be literate? More specifically, for our purpose, what does it mean to teach literacy? The first two chapters begin with the foundations of literacy and language acquisition. Before assuming that literacy instruction begins with teaching the alphabet, we must look into what it means to read and write. This section of the text provides you with a broad understanding of what literacy and language are in relation to young students.

Chapter 1: What is Literacy?

What is literacy? Take a moment to think about how you would define literacy. Most people define literacy by a person's ability to read and write. While this is the most common and popular way to define literacy, literacy goes beyond just reading and writing (Guerra, 1998). Most of us think about learning how to read and write in school, but literacy really begins at home (Morrow, 2001). Over the decades of schooling in the United States, researchers and policy makers have examined reading instruction very closely (National Reading Panel, 2000). Reading tests have been used to measure students, teachers, and schools. Literacy and reading are not necessarily the same thing. In our tutoring program, we highlight the idea of literacy—not just the skill of reading. It will be imperative for you to understand the difference.

Purpose of the Chapter

Literacy is a complex topic and this chapter is designed to provide you with background information on how literacy is defined, what theories are used to describe literacy, and what types of literacies students bring to tutoring. Literacy includes understanding a topic in depth, being able to talk about the topic, and learning more by reading texts, viewing videos, or understanding graphics. Think about a topic you know very well. You may have personal experiences and background knowledge related to the topic. For example, Julie's uncle was a shrimper. His knowledge of the gulf waters, the weather, the shrimp, fish, and oysters he gathered was in-depth. Yes, he could read and write and used these skills when he worked, but he also had to "read" the weather and water, had to know what time of day to head out on the boat, what time of year to fish for flounder, and when to harvest oysters. He was able to analyze laws and legislation that regulated his fishing and respond their influence on his work. He was articulate and very knowledgeable. He could break down his ideas and explain them to others and demonstrate how to prepare the boat, how to fish, and what the signs of the weather and water meant. He was highly literate in fishing and shrimping. On the other hand, we are not literate in fishing. While we can see if the sky is sunny or cloudy, we cannot tell what that means for fishing that day. We can read a book on how to prepare a boat for the water, but we cannot actually walk up to a boat and know how to interpret what we see. All of us have literacies related to our lives. Students bring their literacies to us and we must recognize and use them as we build their reading and writing abilities.

Literacy involves knowing about particular topics in-depth. Julie may have a PhD in literacy but she is not literate in many areas. Julie is not literate about astronomy or taxes. She can read the instructions on her tax return and try to answer each question but she does not really understand deeply what the questions mean. Julie prefers to go to a professional tax accountant for assistance with my taxes because this individual is highly literate in current tax laws and can interpret the tax forms in ways beyond my comprehension. This does not mean Julie cannot read, but it does show how literacy is more than just reading words on a page. We want you to keep this in mind as you tutor. Before you read the chapter, please take a moment to answer the pre-reading questions that follow. Record your answers so when you are done reading you can go back and review what you have learned. Definitions for each term are both in the text and in the glossary.

> ### Pre-Reading Questions
> How would you define literacy?
> How is literacy used by students in their daily lives?

The following terms will be crucial for you to understand as you move into learning how to tutor students.

<table>
<tr><td colspan="4">**Key Terms**</td></tr>
<tr><td>Literacy</td><td>Developmental Level</td><td>Multimodal</td><td>Funds of Knowledge</td></tr>
</table>

Understanding these key terms will help you as you learn about teaching your student. Our goal is make sure you recognize the literacies that students bring to the tutoring sessions so you can build your teaching on their strengths. When students struggle with reading and writing, it helps to know what they are interested in and already know about. For example, if a student knows a lot about dinosaurs, you can build your reading and writing around dinosaurs. The following sections cover theories, developmental levels, types of literacy, and how forces in and outside of schools shape literacy for young students.

What Are Theories Related to Literacy?

Theories are used to define literacy and provide a framework on how to teach literacy (Tracey & Morrow, 2012). While most of us do not talk about theories in our daily lives, we all have theories about how things work and how they should be done. Some people may theorize the best way to train a horse is to use behaviorism and give the horse treats for each command performed correctly. Others may follow a more natural approach and work with the animal's natural behaviors to get the horse to do specific things. Theories guide our thinking. They give us ways to explain how and why we are doing a task in a particular way. We may or may not talk directly about our theories in scholarly terms but they are there and meaningful for us. The same ideas are true for teaching literacy. There are many theories about how to teach students to read and write; some are focused on how to teach the broader ideas related to literacy while others emphasize learning skills such as the alphabet. There are no right or wrong theories; most good instruction uses many aspects of various theories. Each student is different so the more approaches you can use, the more effective you will be. See Tracey & Morrow (2012) for a comprehensive look at the theories related to literacy. Some students need focused direct instruction at times and others may need a more student-centered type of lesson. In our tutoring program, we will present ideas that reflect many theories but the theories we will most rely upon will be: (1) psycholinguistic theory (Goodman, 1967; Smith, 1971), (2) developmental stages of reading development (Fountas & Pinnell, 1996), (3) multimodal literacies (Kress, 2000), and (4) funds of knowledge (Gonzales, Moll, & Amanti, 2005). You do not have to memorize these ideas but you do need to understand their basic components before you begin to tutor.

Thinking about literacy broadly and approaching your instruction from a literacy perspective—rather than just a reading and writing view—means you will recognize the literacies students bring with them and work to build a bridge between what they know and what they need to know instead of just teaching a list of words and skills. The following sections describe the theories related to our views of tutoring.

Literacy

Literacy is a broad term that moves beyond simple reading and writing. Literacy includes in-depth knowledge about a topic, and the ability to listen, speak, read, and write.

What Are Literacies?

"Literacies" refer to all types of literacies students bring to us. At times, there can be a very specific focus on a student's ability to read particular books or write certain words. As we mentioned earlier, there are many types of literacies when you look beyond just reading and writing. It is important to recognize how we can understand a student's strengths. In the example about Julie's uncle the shrimper, you learned how his knowledge went beyond reading words on a page. There are many recognized literacies (Cope & Kalantzis, 2002). Termed multiple literacies, these literacies are identified as scientific literacy, civic literacy, financial literacy, etc. and represent ways to name different types of literacies in relation to specific types of knowledge. Each of these literacies is unique to the area it covers. For example, civic literacy refers to the knowledge and understanding of how to engage in civic life (Marciano, 1997). When we think of civic life we may think of voting or community service. To be civically literate we do not necessarily need to be able to read and write; it is ideal and we would never want someone to not be able to read and write, but it is not a requirement. Citizens can determine how they are going to vote by watching the news, going to town hall meetings, or talking with others to make informed decisions. Even in the earliest of democracies, oral discussion was the predominate mode of engaging in civic acts (Graff, 1987). Other literacies are just as specific and may not depend on just reading and writing. For our purposes, it is important to recognize these types of literacies to know what types our students are bringing to our lessons so we can learn from the students and connect what they know to the printed words they need to be able to read and write. Although we focus on literacy broadly, we are also working with students to ensure they can read and write well. Relying on their existing knowledge can be an effective way to bring reading to life for struggling students.

Funds of Knowledge

Funds of Knowledge

Funds of knowledge stress the important knowledge students bring with them to instructional settings.

"Funds of knowledge" is a concept we will use often in tutoring. Related to multiple literacies, funds of knowledge stress the important knowledge students bring with them to instructional settings (Gonzalez, Moll, & Amanti, 2005). Too often school settings are separated from the home lives of students, with educators expecting that students will conform to school expectations with little regard for their existing knowledge and abilities.

Funds of knowledge is based on research by Moll, Amanti, Neff, & Gonzalez (1992) in which the researchers went into students' homes and brought family and student knowledge into the classroom. They found students were more engaged and learned more than when their knowledge was overlooked (Moll, Amanti, Neff, and Gonzalez, 1992; Gonzalez & Moll, 2002). Students in tutoring programs are often not doing well in school. They may not be motivated to read and write or see how school connects to their own experiences. As you tutor you want to get to know your students and their families so you can build on what they know and see their strengths. We cover this in more detail in Chapter 11.

Multimodal Literacy

Multimodal literacy is a fairly new term. The New London Group (Cope & Kalantzis, 2002) defines multimodal literacy as all the modes of literacy we engage in on a daily basis. Multimodal literacy recognizes the technology we use, the media we read, and views text as more than words in a book. Multimodal literacy expands literacy to the modes we create and consume today—web pages, videos, podcasts, apps, and other forms of media and visual or auditory input. Many of us do not read a book or newspaper to get information. We rely on other modes of gaining information or enjoying entertainment. This matters for teaching reading because we can use various modes to teach students.

Multimodal Literacy

Multimodal literacy recognizes the various texts and modes we use today beyond just books.

Students are already engaged in viewing and creating videos, playing video games, and reading websites with text, graphics, pictures, and videos. Multimodal literacy in tutoring allows us to bring all these modes into our teaching and allows students to make their own videos, blogs using text and visuals, and much more. Utilizing multiple modes of expression keeps students interested and connects their literacy learning to their lives outside of school.

What Are Developmental Levels?

Developmental Levels

Developmental reading levels refer to the predictable stages of reading that young readers go through as they learn to read.

Developmental levels are very important to teaching literacy to young students. Working with elementary students is exciting when you see them making progress quickly. Yet due to the young age of students, it is helpful to look at how readers develop over time. While literacy is broad, developmental levels of reading highlight very specific reading behaviors that you can observe in your student. Most of us think about student reading abilities as they relate to grade level. We expect kindergarteners to learn their ABCs and be able to write the alphabet. We know that first grade is the year reading is taught to students, and that they should be able to read by the end of their first-grade year. Yet, research has shown us over time that grade levels or even student ages do not always fit students. Each student learns at his or her own pace.

Students do not always fit into grade-level expectations. Many kindergarteners can read books on their own and some second graders may still be working on their alphabet sounds. Researchers and instructors (Clay, 1985; Fountas & Pinnell, 1996) have noted that while young students may learn at different rates, they still generally follow a certain path to learning how to read. This path is referred to as the developmental reading level. Please review Table 1.1.

As you read through the chart, note the descriptions and how they increase in complexity over time. Knowing where your student falls in the chart will help you not only to identify their developmental stage, but also to see what types of activities you can plan to help them move to the next stage. The stages are described in ways that are observable. You can observe your student and begin to see where he or she is developmentally. The other assumption behind the developmental levels theory is that most students will progress through each stage in order. In addition to theories on how students learn in stages, developmental stages can help explain how students actually read.

What Is Psycholinguistic Theory?

Psycholinguistic theory applies to our view of tutoring due to its emphasis on the importance of meaning and understanding in reading (Goodman, 1967; Smith, 1971). At times, reading instruction can become disjointed and focus on smaller skills such as sounding out each word. A psycholinguistic view looks at how students use meaning to understand texts. This is compatible with our focus on student literacies and the developmental view of reading development. For example, you may be able to play tennis well when hitting balls coming from a machine. The machine is somewhat predictable; it can be set up to put the ball in a place that is comfortable for you. Being able to hit a tennis ball well when it is coming to you at a predictable speed and placement is one thing; a real tennis game in which your partner will not hit the ball directly toward you is very different. If students are taught one reading skill, such as sounding out words as they read, they will only be partially prepared to read actual texts. Many words, such as *said*, cannot be decoded. Therefore, you want to make sure you are teaching them many ways

Table 1.1 Developmental Reading Levels

	Emergent Readers	Early Readers	Transitional Readers	Self-Extending Readers
Description	• Use mostly information from pictures. • May attend to and use some features of print. • May notice how print is used. • May know some words. • May use the introduced language patterns of books. • May respond to texts by linking meaning to their experiences. • Beginning to make links between their oral language and print.	• Rely less on pictures and use more information from print. • Have increasing control of early reading strategies. • Know several frequently used words. automatically. • Read using more than one source of information. • Read familiar texts with phrasing and fluency. • Exhibit behaviors indicating strategies used as monitoring, searching, cross-checking, and self-correction.	• Have full control of early strategies. • Use multiple sources of information while reading for meaning. • Integrate the use of cues. • Have a large core of frequently used words. • Notice pictures but rely very little on pictures to read the text. • For the most part, read fluently with phrasing. • Read longer, more complex texts.	• Use all course of information flexibly. • Solve problems in an independent way. • Read with phrasing and fluency. • Extend their understanding by reading a wide range of texts for different purposes. • Read for meaning, solving problems in an independent way. • Continue to learn from reading. • Read much longer, more complex texts. • Read a variety of genres.
Age and Grade Range	Approximately ages 2 to 7 Preschool to early Grade 1	Approximately ages 5 to 7 Kindergarten to Grade 1	Approximately ages 5 to 7 Kindergarten to Grade 2	Approximately ages 6 to 9 Grades 1 to 3

(Clay, 1985; Fountas & Pinnell, 1996)

to read, just as a good tennis coach will work with you not only with the ball machine but also with an actual partner.

Psycholinguistic theory explains how readers use cueing systems as they read: (1) meaning/semantics, (2) grammar/syntax, and (3) visual/graphophonic (Goodman, 1967; Smith, 1971). Each cueing system is used by all readers. We all rely on sounding out words, using our knowledge of grammar and what we know about the meaning of the text we are reading. These three systems are automatic and occur very quickly and automatically in good readers, but for developing and struggling readers, they are not used efficiently or only one is used. Our goal is to recognize the value of the three cueing systems and teach them to students who are still learning how to read. For example, you may see some students who have been taught that reading is sounding out every word. While this is a very important part of reading and helps us to read unknown words, it is just one aspect of reading. There can be significant problems if this is the only reading strategy used, especially since words such as *the*, *know*, or *saw* cannot be sounded out successfully. Reading the sentence that follows will be extremely difficult for readers who only know how to decode words letter by letter.

I saw the cat.

For a reader who only knows how to read by decoding, the words *saw* and *the* will be problematic; *the* and *saw* are not words a reader can sound out letter by letter. If a reader can use his or her knowledge of grammar and meaning, they will be able to read the sentence. The grammatical structure of the sentence is familiar to English speakers. The order of the words is a common sentence pattern. The word *cat* is decodable and the reader could use meaning to put all the words together. As is often the case with beginning level books, visual support with pictures can assist students with using meaning based on the picture. Psycholinguistic theory explains the importance of sounding out words, using grammar and meaning together in order to read. The terms used to delineate each cue are in table 1.2:

Table 1.2   Reading Cueing Systems

Semantics (Meaning)	Syntax (Grammar)	Decoding (Visual)
Relying on the meaning of the text.	Relying on the grammatical structure of the text.	Relying on the letter/sound decoding of the text and pictures.

(Goodman, 1967; Smith, 1971)

All three of these cueing systems work together as we read. Our goal is to develop each one in struggling readers so they can become independent readers.

Who Defines and Shapes Literacy in and out of School?

While we set up our tutoring program to embrace broad, multiple types and modes of literacy based on student knowledge, there are many stakeholders involved in literacy education. Students' literacy experiences are shaped by the ideas of their families, their schools, and their communities. These areas are essential to understand because some students' learning is molded by the contexts of their lives. Since students' literacy is influenced by family, school, and community, it is important for you to be aware of your student's literacy.

Literacy Leaders: Families

Families are the first literacy teachers for their children. We discuss the significance of families in detail in Chapter 11, but for now it is important to learn how families influence students' oral language, grammar usage, topic knowledge, and love or concerns about reading and writing. Knowing how families engage in literacy, how they read and talk with their children, and what types of experiences they have is key to providing relatable lessons to your student. Early on in your tutoring program, you will want to get to know your student's family and what the parents or guardians want for their child.

School Literacy

Schools are also a very strong influence on students' literacy. Some schools rely on a psycholinguistic view of reading; others may use more behaviorist phonics programs to teach reading. Knowing how your student has been taught to read is crucial. Some students may try to sound out each word because that is what they were taught, while others may guess at unknown words and not use the letter sounds. Knowing this can help you talk to students about other strategies they can use. Depending on your tutoring program, it can be difficult to learn about your student's schooling and you will have to be careful not to violate privacy laws. You may, however, ask your student how he or she learned to read and what was read in school. Most students can describe the types of books read in school and the activities they took part in.

Essential Elements of Literacy

As you can see, literacy is a broad and complex topic. As you tutor, the following essential elements will be important to remember as you learn about tutoring:

1. All students possess literacy related to their background knowledge and experiences.

2. Teaching literacy takes theory, student knowledge, and developmental levels into account.

3. Literacy includes reading, writing, listening, and speaking.

4. Literacy is multimodal and goes beyond books and pen and paper.

All of these elements are important to tutoring and you will want to keep them in mind. Students need to be the center of your instruction as you plan for their unique developmental levels and knowledge.

Summary

Teaching students how to read and write using their existing literacies is an important job. The complex definitions and theories cited in this chapter will be used throughout the book. The lesson plans and detailed explanations of activities are all aligned with these ideas. You will see activities connected to real world modes of learning, be asked to get to know your students and their families, and of course how to teach specific reading and writing strategies so your student can become highly literate. Please revisit the pre-reading questions to check and revise your initial answers.

Pre-Reading Questions

How is literacy defined?

What types of literacies do you possess?

Clarify why you should know about your student's literacy as you teach.

Chapter 2: What Do You Know About Language and Literacy?

What do you know about language and literacy acquisition? If you are reading this, you obviously can read English. Do you remember how you learned to speak and read? As you think about language and literacy, think about your own literacy journey. What literacy practices did you take part in as a child, at home, in school, and in the community?

Before you read this chapter, please take a moment to answer the questions that follow. Record your answers in the KWL chart (Ogle, 1986), listing how you learned and what you would like to learn about literacy. And finally, when you are finished reading, not just this chapter but the entire book, you can go back and list what you have learned.

Table 2.1

Know	Want to Learn	Learned
What do I know about how I learned how to talk?		
What do I know about how I learned how to read?		
What do I know about how I learned how to write?		

Do you remember learning about these areas? Many of us do not. Language acquisition is a natural process that typically occurs without specific instruction.

Purpose of the Chapter

The purpose of this chapter is to assist you in understanding the complex process of language and literacy acquisition. The general assumption for many is to see literacy as the process of encoding and decoding print or reading and writing. Is that how you answered the question "what does literacy mean?" This would not be completely incorrect but it would also not be the complete picture of what is involved in literacy. Literacy is a complex process that we often oversimplify to mean being able to read and write. As teachers and tutors, we think of our job as helping students to learn to read and write, but to successfully assist students in the process there are other factors we need to consider. Go back and reflect on your literacy journey we asked you to answer earlier. What are your memories of literacy practices from childhood? Do you remember being read to by a parent, grandparent, older sibling, or other caregiver at home? Did you have a bedtime story ritual? Do you remember a favorite book that was read to you over and over, read so much that you had memorized large portions of the text? Were there songs or rhymes you remember hearing at home? Think about your community literacy memories too. Did you go to story time at the local library or at a bookstore? Did you attend church school with your family where you may have been read stories, taught songs, or been involved in other story time activities?

All of these are important oral literacy events that helped form your understanding of language and literacy as a child even before you entered formal schooling. These familial and social language practices help build the literacy blocks needed to begin an understanding of literacy at school for students. As a tutor, it is important that you understand your student's home, school, and community language and literacy background. You cannot assume your student will share the same home, school, and community literacy background as you, so getting to know your student's literacy story is important to being a successful tutor.

Pre-Reading Questions

What does it mean to acquire language?
How do students learn to read and write?

Several key terms will be important as you meet your student and begin working with him or her. Understanding the components involved in language and literacy acquisition and their use will be discussed throughout the chapter.

Key Terms

Nonstandard Variety of English	Dialect	Language Register	English Learners

---

Each term is defined for you and specific definitions will be highlighted within the text. As you begin to tutor, you will be able to use these terms to describe your student's language and literacy abilities.

Oral Language and Literacy

Before you learned to read or write you were exposed to a plethora of language events and practices at home and in your community, whether you were aware of this or not. Even before you learned to talk, you were bombarded by thousands of sounds, rhythms, and words that as a young child you may have tried to imitate. As your language began to develop into clear words, simple phrases, and eventually more complex sentences that supported your thought processes your ability to verbally communicate with those around you grew and your message was acknowledged (i.e., "cookie" "I cookie" "I want cookie" was usually rewarded by receiving a cookie for each utterance, Lindfors, 2008). While many of the students we will work with may come from a home where a standard variety of English is spoken, or the form of English accepted in the school environment (Corson, 1997; Schleppegrell, 2004), we will also have students who come to the program where a nonstandard variety of English, or a language other than English is spoken at home or in their community. You will need to understand the complexity of your student's language experience and how to build upon what he or she brings to the tutoring environment; students offer an enormous amount of information and knowledge about their communication style. Thus, tapping into it and making connections to the language of school is part of the tutoring task. Let us first discuss language varieties, and then English learners who speak a first language other than English to begin to understand the language capabilities students bring with them.

Please view the video and notice the student's oral language patterns.

Video 2.1

Nonstandard Varieties of English

Lave and Wenger (1991) argue we are all members of communities of practice, and participation in these communities informs our language use and identity. Some of the students who will come to the tutoring program are from homes or communities where they have experienced a nonstandard variety of English.

These students may have heard this form of English spoken since birth and have adopted this as their home language and as the language in which they successfully navigate their home and community environments. While this language variation may not be familiar to you, it is still a complex form of communication with its own rules and registers.

Dialect

While students may use a nonstandard variety of English to communicate at home, they may have some exposure to traditional "school" English through media, TV shows, or other language experiences prior to attending school. To assume they do not have any skills upon which to build on would be incorrect. Halliday (1993) tells us that "language is the essential condition of knowing, the process by which experience becomes knowledge" (p. 94). Halliday is talking about all forms of language and not just the language privileged by schools. For example, being from Texas, Julie speaks a specific dialect in which the following sentence would be considered correct.

I'm fixin' to go to the store.

Fixin' is a word used often and regularly in Texas. Dialects are specific to particular communities and are considered to be correct forms of language. They have consistent grammatical rules and vocabulary just as standard American English does. Corson (1997) explains the existence of language variations as a result of "historical divisions, different patterns of behavior, differences in power and differences in language experience "(p. 236). The sentence above is grammatically correct and the usage and pronunciation of the word *fixin'* is consistently applied in this particular Texas dialect. Although Julie can speak standard American English whenever she wants, when Julie is in Texas with friends and family, Julie uses the dialect the community uses. It is the job of you, the tutor, to learn about and build upon students' language experiences and practices and add to their language repertoire without asking them to replace their own dialect with the standard form. The difference between you and your student who may speak a nonstandard form of English is that you have had years of schooling, and have developed the ability to go back and forth in use of the appropriate form of English depending on the context.

Register

Language register refers to the levels of language we use in relation to formality (Joos, 1961). Think about all the different varieties of the English language you may have been exposed to and used depending on the context or situation. Do you have a certain group of friends who speak very casually and use slang with one another? Or maybe at home, where you and your family are so comfortable with one another that you may not even use complete sentences to communicate. In these instances, you have developed and used various registers of English from formal, consultative, to casual or intimate (Joos, 1961). This basically means we use different forms of language to speak to different audiences, and this can play a significant role in teaching.

Students who have not been exposed to the more formal forms of English such as found in some texts may struggle with the grammatical structure and vocabulary of standard English. Think of how you may invite your best friend out to dinner versus how you might ask your town's mayor to a formal reception. You would use different forms of English to complete both tasks.

As educators, we must value the language the student brings with him or her to the tutoring session. We build upon the language knowledge and skills the student brings, and through tutoring can begin to add the standard forms and functions necessary to be successful in "school talk." As a tutor you should put aside any preconceived ideas or stereotypes you may have because the student speaks a nonstandard form of English. We look at the language skills a student brings to tutoring as an asset, and then expand the student's language repertoire through modeling, authentic communication skills, and a variety of reading and writing events used throughout the sessions. In addition to students who speak a variation of English, we will also tutor students who come from home environments in which a language other than English is spoken.

Language Registers

Language registers are the different types of styles used depending on context and audience.

English Learner

An English learner (EL) is a student whose first or home language is a language other than English and who most often relies on that language to successfully communicate.

English Learners

The term *English learners* (ELs) is used to describe students who are enrolled in U.S. schools and use a language (or languages) other than English as their main form of communication at home, in the community, and often in school. ELs, many of whom are born in the United States (Zinshteyn, 2014), may have well-developed social English-language skills but still need assistance developing their academic English abilities to be successful in school. There is a growing group of EL students who come to tutoring with a wide range of English-language skills and abilities. As tutors, it is important to learn your students' home-language abilities and their English skills. One can start by asking "getting-to-know-you questions," such as: Do they speak mainly in the home language at home, in the community? Do they read and write in the home language? Which language do they feel more comfortable using in talking to friends and family members? If they play a sport outside of school, which language is used at practice and on the field? Which language do they prefer using when they are on the school playground with friends? These and a variety of other questions can be asked to better understand your student's language experiences. A questionnaire with these and other questions can be found below.

Other information that would assist you in better understanding your student's language skills is knowing how long he or she has been in a U.S. school, how long the student may have attended school in the home country, and whether English-language instruction was part of the curriculum in the home country. You may teach K-6 EL students who have been in U.S. schools for a few months (students from Mexico), or a year or two (students from China), or students who have spent their entire school experience in U.S. schools. Speaking a home language other than English does not mean a student was not born in the United States. Students who come to tutoring will have varying amounts of exposure to U.S. schooling, which makes getting to know your student—and his or her literacy needs—paramount. We acknowledge the languages our students bring with them as assets, and create lesson plans to assist them in gaining and building their English skills while encouraging them to continue using their home language. By asking your students specific questions about their talents and ability to speak multiple languages and inquiring about their reading and writing habits, you can begin to select appropriate and engaging materials for your lessons. The following language and literacy questionnaire can assist you in beginning the process of getting to know your student's language abilities. Remember, the more you know about your student's language experiences the more information you will have to craft appropriate and engaging lessons.

Language and Literacy Questionnaire— Getting to Know Your Student

The following questions can be used as a guide as you get to know your student. You can select the questions you believe are most appropriate for him or her. This is just one way to get to know your student better. After you have discussed these questions with your student, you can have the student ask you the same questions about your language and literacy skills so he or she can learn more about you too. Also, it is a great way to share your own language experience with the student and for you to think about your literacy journey. When the tutoring session ends it is important to reflect on what you have learned about your student so you can focus on his or her language and literacy strengths and the student's literacy needs, and then begin planning the lesson for your next session. A reflection guide is provided in Appendix 2.2.

Table 2.2

Possible Questions to Ask	Response
Which languages do you speak at home?	
Which languages do you use in the neighborhood and your community?	
How many different languages do you speak?	
Which languages do you use to read and write when you are at home or in the community?	
Which language do you feel more comfortable using to talk to friends and family members?	
If you play a sport outside of school which language is used at practice and on the field?	
Which language do you prefer using when you are on the school playground with friends?	
Would you prefer to read a book in your home language or in English?	
If you were reading a book in your home language where on the page would you start reading?	
Do you enjoy reading for fun?	
Do you read at home?	
What types of materials, books, or stories do you like to read?	
Do you ever read aloud to others or younger children at school or in the community?	
Do you enjoy being read to?	
Who reads to you at home (or used to read to you when you were younger)?	
Where do you go to get books to read at home?	

Please view the video of a student responding to the questionnaire.

Video 2.2

One question we would never ask EL students is one regarding their own or their family's legal status in this country. Our goal is to learn about their literacy so we can teach them well. It is hoped this questionnaire will help you develop a better picture of your student's literacy background. Remember that not every student will have the same literacy background. You learned in Chapter 1 about the rich and diverse funds of knowledge that can be found in your student's home and community. This source of literacy knowledge may come in many forms, such as a rich oral tradition that would expose your student to wonderful cultural folktales, legends, myths, or family stories passed down through storytelling. Or you may have a student whose literacy exposure is through hearing Bible stories read aloud, or reading recipes to help prepare family meals, or perhaps they read technical manuals to help fix a computer or other mechanical items in the household (Gonzalez, Moll, & Amanti, 2005). Not every household has traditional children's books to read but that does not mean the household is not rich in language and literacy experiences. Rachel did not grow up in a house full of children's literature. Her father had a beautiful leather-bound set of poetry. The poetry, written by American and British poets, was filled with images of war ("The Charge of the Light Brigade" by Alfred Lord Tennyson) and death ("O Captain! My Captain!" by Walt Whitman). Her father read from these books every night; he had memorized many of the poems and sonnets and would recite them to anyone in the house who would listen. Rachel's mother, on the other hand, was an oral storyteller. All of her stories were told in Spanish. She shared many of the legends and myths she heard growing up in Mexico, some of them quite frightening! while Rachel did not grow up reading Dr. Seuss, she did grow up in a language-rich environment hearing words in both English and Spanish that provided incredible images and a cacophony of sounds. Rachel and her siblings grew up to become avid and voracious readers. Your job as a tutor is to learn what types of language and literacy knowledge your student brings to the tutoring session and build a bridge to link their home and community literacy to school literacy practices. By now you should have a much better picture of the necessary components involved in understanding what literacy means. Another important element in the development of literacy, and one we have addressed indirectly throughout this chapter, is the social aspect of literacy. Throughout this chapter we have discussed language and the need to know the language skills our student brings from home, the community, and school to the tutoring session. Language is integral to reading, writing, and communicating and cannot be omitted from the definition of literacy. Literacy is a social act informed by the cultural practices of the participants (Street, 2005).

Social View of Literacy

At the beginning of this chapter you were asked what you knew about language and literacy. Within the chapter is a discussion of the inextricable link between language and literacy and the different forms and styles of language used by students to access literacy within their home and communities. Take a moment now and think about what you know about literacy and see if you can come up with a concrete definition of what literacy means to you. It is not easy to put into words because it is a complex and dynamic process. A traditional view of literacy, one many of you may be familiar with, would define literacy as the process of reading and writing, decoding and encoding to make meaning from text that conveys a message through a visual format and process that occurs with an individual

(Gee, 2015; Hawkins, 2013). Where is the interplay of language and cultural context, experience, and understanding in this definition? As addressed earlier in this chapter, these are important components to literacy as well. To understand a definition of literacy that includes not just reading, writing, and language, but the cultural, political, and economic practices (Gee, 2015, Street, 2013) that inform literacy, a social view of literacy is needed. We know literacy includes reading (decoding) and writing (encoding) at a basic level. What are the purposes for reading? Do students read just to pass a test and advance to the next level? Why do students write the five-paragraph essay? Does writing this essay in some way advance students beyond the concrete walls and linoleum halls of schools? A definition of literacy should include an understanding of the social interactions and practices used by students in their daily life. How and where does your student use literacy? How and where do you use literacy? What modalities are used to express our literate self? All of these questions can be answered by looking at the social aspect of literacy events. As members of various language and literacy communities (school, social groups, book clubs, online communities, etc.), the interactions between and among participants help shape our identity as active learners who gain knowledge from the social transactions of literacy (Hawkins, 2013). If students have a specific purpose for engaging in active literacy practices within social learning communities and can call upon their previous literacy experiences to build new knowledge, it is more likely they will successfully develop their literacy skills. The goal of tutoring is to help our students set a purpose for learning and assist them in developing their language and literacy abilities. To do this, you should be committed to constant communication with the student's family and including them as part of the student's community of learning.

Communicating with Families About Literacy

It is not only essential to understand how family literacy events or funds of knowledge inform the student's literacy growth and development, but maintaining open communication with the family is also important. Families can provide us with vital information on how best to work with their children. To achieve this home/school connection we recommend that you communicate with families as much as possible. Your first interaction with the family should be welcoming so you can get to know the student and his or her family. Ask them questions; let them know you want to know about their child so you can work with them. You should continue to talk with the family as you tutor, letting the family know what you are doing and why. You should ask the parents or guardians what goals they have for their child in the program. Students should also be asked to set goals for their tutoring experience. We will discuss working with families in detail in Chapter 11.

Summary

Understanding the rich literacy practices—often different from our own—that your student's family uses at home and within the community is essential in assisting the student in achieving school literacy skills. Furthermore, acknowledging the language skills all students have and bringing them to the classroom discourse aids you in designing and creating appropriate lesson plans for tutoring. Finally, situating language and literacy as inseparable entities within a social model of literacy will help you in developing engaging lessons. Take a moment to return to the K-W-L chart and reflect upon what you have learned about literacy. Continue to use the chart as you read on and gain more knowledge about literacy and literacy practices. Please review and revise your initial answers to the re-reading questions.

Pre-Reading Questions

What type of dialect do you use? Where did your oral language patterns come from? How have they influenced your reading and writing?

What is the importance of oral language?

Identify some of the important components to developing literacy skills for ELs.

PART II: TUTORING KNOWLEDGE

Understanding the foundations of literacy instruction and assessment is key to being an effective tutor. In this section, we cover the various aspects of reading and writing and how they are broken down and defined for instruction. We also share some of the basic ways each area is taught and assessed.

Chapter 3: What Do You Need to Know to Teach Literacy?

What do you need to know about literacy to teach it? As we stated in the previous chapters, literacy is more than just reading and writing. Yet as a literacy tutor, you do have to be aware of how literacy is broken down into smaller components. Researchers have spent decades exploring, categorizing, and studying not only literacy, but how to break literacy down into specific areas to teach. Traditionally, literacy instruction has focused on listening, speaking, reading, and writing. There are many curricular materials, lesson structures, and assessments designed to target each area as students learn to increase their content and skills knowledge. As a tutor, you need to understand both the content of literacy and also the pedagogical content of literacy (Shulman, 1986). The content of literacy instruction at the elementary level is dedicated to the specific components of reading and writing; the pedagogical content knowledge of literacy is centered on how to actually teach those areas of literacy. For example, think of something you know how to do well. Even though you may be very good at the activity, you may not be able to teach someone else how to do it. When Julie was younger, she went water skiing with friends. They told her to just hang onto the ski rope and then let the boat pull her up out of the water. After nearly drinking the entire lake, she was no closer to learning to ski than before she got into the water hours earlier. The next day one of the parents in our group was able to explain to her that she needed to keep her knees bent and keep them together, make sure her arms were straight, and maintain a sitting position as she was pulled by the boat. These tips were all she needed to be able to water ski. While my friends were correct in that Julie needed to allow the boat to pull her up out of the water, they neglected to tell her how to position her knees and arms so she could be successful. The same principle is true in teaching anything to someone. It is helpful if the teacher is able to do the activity being taught but it is most important they are able to break down the activity to meet the needs of the learner. This is the essence of tutoring. You may be able to read and write, of course, but you must also be able to explain how to read and write to your student. This chapter will unpack each element of literacy and how to teach it so that your students can be successful.

Purpose of the Chapter

The purpose of this chapter is to introduce you to the basic components of literacy and how to teach them. We will separate literacy into two broad categories: (1) reading, and (2) writing. Listening and speaking are also extremely important in literacy and in literacy learning. They will consistently be a part of our tutoring sessions and are embedded into the lesson structures. Our focus here will look at the separate components of reading and writing, how they are defined, and how they are taught. The following key terms will be covered in detail.

Key Terms

Content Knowledge	Comprehension	Phonemic Awareness	Word study
	Accuracy		
Pedagogical Content Knowledge	Fluency	Phonics	
		Vocabulary	

All of these terms are related to literacy and specifically literacy instruction. We want you to be able to identify them and be able to understand all of the ways they can be taught to young learners. The following sections will explain and provide examples connected to each area of literacy. Before you read this chapter, please take a moment to answer the pre-reading questions that follow. Record your answers so when you are done reading you can go back and review what you have learned.

Pre-Reading Questions

How would you teach someone to read?
How would you teach someone to write?

Content Knowledge

Content Knowledge refers to the foundational knowledge of the field or discipline taught. (Shulman, 1986)

What Content Knowledge Do I Need to Know about Literacy?

Knowing what the components of literacy are is key. Your content knowledge is important and you will learn to rely on your understanding as you teach. There are many literacy programs that want teachers to rely on scripts and prepared lessons that cover each area, but we want you to have a foundation of knowledge so you can make your own teaching decisions based on how your student is learning. To do that, you have to have a strong command of what reading and writing are. This content knowledge (Shulman, 1986) is key to teaching literacy.

Knowing the basic areas of literacy will enable you to make decisions about your instruction that are well informed and appropriate for your student. The areas we will highlight are detailed in the following sections.

What is reading?

Reading is complex. For our purposes, we rely on three major aspects of reading in the tutoring program. Word recognition is the reader's ability to read words accurately. Comprehension is the understanding of the text read and fluency is the reading rate and expression of the reader. All of these areas combine as a reader reads any text.

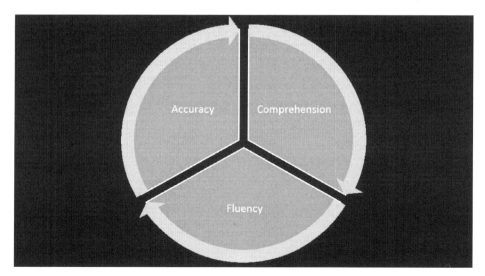

Comprehension

Comprehension

Comprehension is making meaning from text.

Comprehension simply means understanding (Rumelhart, 1984). Even though it seems to be a commonsense idea, many times struggling readers have difficulty with comprehension as they read. Comprehension in relation to reading can be quite complex. For our purposes, we will focus on three types of comprehension: (1) literal, (2) inferential, and (3) critical.

Literal comprehension can be described as "reading the lines" of text. For example, read the following text:

The little girl was crying because she lost her sister.

What does this statement mean? If you were asked what happened in this sentence, what would you say? Most of us would say the little girl was crying. This is a very literal restatement of what the sentence states. Often readers are able to restate parts of the texts they read and demonstrate literal understanding of what they read. Literal understanding is defined as the simplest and most direct form of comprehension. It is usually the easiest type of comprehension for young readers. One thing to note as you work with reading comprehension is to be cautious about making sure readers are not just restating what they read verbatim. You want them to put their literal understanding into their own words. So, if a reader said, "The little girl was crying because she had lost her sister," you would want to ask of the reader what that means in his or her own words. There is a difference between reciting text from memory and putting the meaning of the text into one's own words.

Inferential comprehension goes beyond explaining the text on the page. Inferencing requires the reader to go beyond the text or "read between the lines." This means the reader has to understand the larger meaning of what he or she is listening to or reading to figure out what is happening. For example, in the following sentence,

A tear ran down the little girl's cheek as she thought of her lost sister.

Here, if you ask the reader what happened in the text, the reader might restate the text. But if you asked how the little girl was feeling, the reader would have to infer the little girl was feeling sad. The text does not explicitly state she is sad, so readers have to deduce based on the entire story or sentence how she is feeling. Inferential comprehension is more complex and asks more of readers than a simple understanding of events and key ideas. Inferencing asks readers to understand beyond the text on the page.

Critical comprehension is dedicated to examining the ideas, characters, and events in a text in relation to outside sources and ideas. Critical comprehension asks students to evaluate or synthesize ideas in the text. For example, in the following sentence,

The little girl called the police to ask them to help her look for her sister.

To engage readers in critical thinking about the text, you would ask them to connect the text to another text, additional outside information, or evaluate the little girl's actions. Thinking critically about a text requires readers to not only see and understand the information in the text, but to delve deeper and connect and evaluate what they understand. Being able to determine whether the little girl in the text did the right thing can depend on using background knowledge or other information from another text. Critical comprehension should go beyond just an opinion about the text; it should include references and identification of the tools used to analyze the reading.

Please view the video to see examples of students' demonstrating their comprehension.

videos 3.1 & 3.2 & 3.3

Accuracy

Comprehension always plays a role in reading but accuracy is important. Accuracy refers to how many words are correctly read. It is important to look at reading accuracy as students read to determine how they are reading. Accuracy is only one part of reading, but it is the easiest to observe. Listening to a reader read and watching which words they are able to read and which ones they cannot is the basic part of reading.

Typically, when readers are able to read all or most of the words in a text they are generally seen as being able to read. Reading accuracy can be calculated and reading success can be measured by the percentage of words read correctly in any given text. Reading a text with 100% accuracy means that every word was read correctly and there were no mistakes. When a reader can read a text with no mistakes, that text is considered to be an independent text. On the other hand, reading between 90% and 97% accuracy puts the text and reader in a readable range, sometimes called an instructional level of reading. Missing more than 20% of the words in a text makes the text a frustration level text and too difficult for the reader.

Accuracy

Accuracy is the number of words read correctly.

Table 3.1

Independent Level Text	Instructional Level Text	Frustration Level Text
100%–98% accuracy	97%–90% accuracy	89% accuracy and below
Students should read independent level texts often.	Students should read instructional level texts with substantial teacher support.	Students should not read frustration level texts.

Accuracy is how accurately readers read the words on the page. For our purposes, we are relying on a psycholinguistic view of reading (Smith, 1971; Goodman, 1967. See Chapter 1). The focus on reading strategies is built on the idea that students use three cueing systems as they read: (1) semantic, (2) syntactic, and (3) visual/graphophonic. Good readers use all of these cueing systems as they read.

Please view the video to see examples of students' reading.

video 3.4 & 3.5

Fluency

The rate and expression readers use as they read is fluency (Kuhn, Schwanwnflugel, Meisinger, Levy, Rasinski, 2010). Reading should sound like talking. This means that how fast readers read and how they use their voice demonstrates their accuracy and comprehension. Rate as connected to fluency is defined as how fast readers read. There are ways to measure rate when readers read aloud and when they read silently. According to Hasbrouck and Tindal (2005), the average rate of reading aloud for a fourth grader is 123 words correct per minute (wcpm). For elementary-aged children (first to fifth grade) the reading aloud rate is between 53–139 wcpm. Some readers can read incredibly fast and not comprehend the text while others may read slowly and have good understanding of what they are reading.

Fluency is also defined by the expression, or prosody, of the reader. Pitch, stress, and intonation while reading are related to how readers pause, raise their voice, and use different tones to indicate questions, excitement, or anger. Fluency is important to reading and is related to how readers understand text and how accurately they read. Slow word-by-word reading can be an indication the text is too difficult. Fluency is also related to the difficulty of the text and how many times it has been read. You will on occasion want students to reread text, just as when you are learning to play a song on an instrument, you rehearse until you can play it fluently the way it was meant to be played. Fluent reading improves when students are allowed to read independent level texts.

Please view the video to see examples of students' fluency. Video 3.7 shows a disfluent reader.

video 3.6 & 3.7

Vocabulary

Knowing words and their meanings is another key component to reading. Vocabulary knowledge allows readers to both decode and recognize words and word parts, and to know what words mean within the text. A broad knowledge of vocabulary can help readers be successful. One way to think about vocabulary is to look at a tiered system (Beck, McKeown, Kucan, 2002).

Tier One words are those used frequently and common in oral language and in reading, words such as *cat, the, happy,* etc. Tier Two words are those that are more complex and do not occur as often, words such as *fortunate, industrious,* etc. Tier Three words are more elusive. They include jargon words and vocabulary specific to certain topics such as science (*osmosis*) and math (*coefficient*). In all, the words readers come across in texts vary by their level of familiarity and difficulty. Depending on the text, it is important to be aware of the types of words readers will see as they read.

Please see the video for an example of a student working on vocabulary.

video 3.8 & 3.9

Phonemic Awareness

Phonemic awareness is the ability to understand how sounds in words work (Juel, Griffith, Gough, 1986). Phonemic awareness does not center on how letters and sounds are related, it is very specifically focused on what sounds are heard in words and how they can be separated and orally manipulated.

For example, the word *cat*. *Cat* is made up of three distinct sounds, or phonemes, /c/, /a/, /t/. We can say each sound separately. We can also remove the /c/ and replace it with the sound /m/ to make a new group of sounds, /m/ /a/ /t/ and a new word. Knowing how to break words apart by sounds and add and remove sounds to make new words is fundamental to phonemic awareness. Phonemic awareness is something that many toddlers still learning language can hear and identify. It typically shows up in rhymes and songs. Young children can begin to hear if words rhyme or not. This is not the only indicator of phonemic awareness but it is often the first sign. Phonemic awareness is considered to be key to reading and to future reading success, but it is not a requirement.

Please see the video for an example of a student demonstrating phonemic awareness.

Phonemic Awareness

Phonemic awareness is the ability to hear and segment sounds in words orally.

video 3.10

Phonics

Phonics

Phonics is understanding the relationship between letters and sounds.

Phonics moves beyond phonemic awareness and includes the letter and sound relationship. Readers need to know the sounds each letter and each spelling pattern make so they can use the sounds to decode words in text. Readers would need to know that the letter *C* makes the /c/ sound and that *A* makes the /a/ sound, etc.

They need to know that each sound can be blended to make the word *cat*. Students also need to understand blends, digraphs, root words, prefixes, suffixes, and inflectional endings. Phonics is the key to decoding text but it has many limitations due to the irregularity of words in English. Some words such as *they* cannot be sounded out letter by letter. Overall, all of these components of reading combine as readers read, with each one crucial to the reading process. Overall, reading consists of all these areas. We can teach them individually but in the end, readers use them together as they read.

Please see the video for an example of a student using phonics.

video 3.11

Writing

Writing is, of course, the act of putting ideas onto paper, or a screen, etc. In literacy instruction, writing is most often seen as a process encased within certain genres or products. Process writing follows the steps most writers complete as they write: (1) prewriting, (2) drafting, (3) revising, (4) editing, and (5) publishing (Graves, 2005). Each stage of writing is viewed as crucial in developing the skills and attitudes about writing that students need. Prewriting involves reading, discussing, drawing, or thinking about the topic and genre goal. Drafting includes getting down ideas quickly and efficiently without too much attention to conventions such as spelling and punctuation. Revision is the process of altering ideas, elaborating on sections, or rearranging areas in the draft. The revision process can occur multiple times. After revisions are completed, the focus turns to editing for spelling, grammar, and punctuation. After all of the phases are worked through, the piece should be read for the final phase of the writing process, which is publication. Not all writing projects need to go through all of the stages; often students may do several drafts and then select one piece of writing to work through to publication. Now that you have an idea of the various components of reading and writing, it is time to examine the ways they can be taught.

Please see the video for an example of a student working through the stages of writing.

video 3.12

What Pedagogical Content Knowledge Do I Need to Know to Teach Literacy?

Pedagogical content knowledge refers to how to teach content (Shulman, 1986). Just as in the example earlier, knowing how to water ski does not guarantee you can teach someone how to ski. Pedagogical content knowledge is the in-depth understanding of an area that enables you to break it down and explain it, provide clear examples, or model it in ways that help someone learn the information successfully.

Once you know the basic ideas behind reading, it is time to learn how to teach readers who are struggling. The term pedagogy means to teach. Thus, pedagogical knowledge is the knowledge of how to teach. Teaching is complex; it requires knowing how to break ideas and skills down into manageable steps. It also requires adjusting to what learners need as they master specific tasks. The following sections provide an overview of some of the ways to teach reading to students.

Types of Reading Instruction

The four main types of reading instruction are detailed in this section. Each type is used to teach specific areas and skills. Reading aloud to students is beneficial for learning about vocabulary, different genres, and for developing student interest in reading. Any level of book can be used as long you, the tutor, can read it. Shared reading, or echo reading, is used to assist students as they read. You and the student read the text together so you can provide support. The book for this activity should be challenging, but not too difficult so the student can follow along. Guided reading involves coaching the reader as he or she reads a challenging book by offering prompts and support. Finally, independent reading allows students to read books that are easy for them.

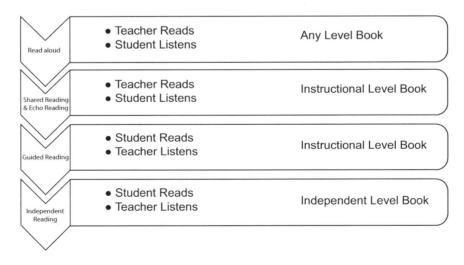

Fig 3.5:

Each of these instructional frames will be covered in detail in later chapters. In the next sections we describe all of the areas related to reading that can be incorporated within the four types of reading activities.

Comprehension

Teaching comprehension is essentially posing questions and setting a purpose for readers before, during, and after reading. While there are many ways to work on readers' comprehension, we will highlight ways to address comprehension within a typical tutoring session. Comprehension instruction during tutoring will highlight the instructional methods used with reading aloud (Chapter 5) and guided reading (Chapter 6). When reading aloud to readers, comprehension instruction is focused on listening comprehension. One way to address comprehension is to break instruction into the three areas of before, during, and after. Before reading, you want to set a purpose for reading by asking the reader to pay attention to a specific aspect of the book or text being read. For instance, you may want to ask the reader to attend to literary elements such as focusing on a certain character or to the conflict in a story. You can also ask the reader to predict what the story will be about or to make connections to text by looking at the picture on the cover or the title of the story. During reading, it is important to ask questions to assess how the reader is understanding the information. Again, you can have students make connections to what they have read. After reading, you can ask the learner to retell the story, confirm his or her predictions, or focus on the purpose you set at the beginning of the activity. These same instructional methods can be used during guided and independent reading when students are reading. These will be covered in more detail in later chapters.

Table 3.2

Reading Comprehension Instruction	Strategies
Before	Set a purpose for reading. Make predictions. Make connections to the title or cover picture. Focus on literary elements. Anticipation guide (answer true/false questions about the story prior to reading) Think-pair-share (provide a prompt)
During	Use Sticky Notes to write thoughts, ideas, questions, connections, or wonderings as they read. Reread parts for clarification. Check and modify predictions. Anticipation guide (take note of true/false answers as they read)
After	Retell or summarize. Confirm predictions. Anticipation guide (check true/false answers) Think-pair-share (answer prompt)

Accuracy

Assisting students with accuracy is complex. Most people want to simply tell readers the words they do not know as they read. While helpful for the moment, telling students the words do not provide them with the necessary skills and strategies to learn how to work through texts on their own. As we mentioned in the previous section, the three cueing systems are important for readers to understand. As you teach you use prompts to help students use all three cueing systems as they read.

Table 3.3

Cueing System	Meaning/Semantics	Syntax/Grammar	Visual/Decoding
Prompts	Did that make sense?	What would sound right?	What does the word begin with?

Beginning and struggling readers tend to rely on one or two cueing systems and therefore need help learning how to use them all successfully. As a tutor, it is important to assess students as they read and be prepared to prompt them to use the cueing systems as they read for more detailed information. Accuracy can also be improved by having students reread the text.

Fluency

As students read, fluency can be taught in several ways: modeling, shared reading, and rereading. Modeling fluency means explaining how students should read a specific sentence or text and then actually demonstrating how to read for them. In shared reading, or sometimes called the neurological impress method, you ask the reader to read along with you as you read with expression at an appropriate pace. One of the most common and effective ways to improve reading fluency is to have students reread texts they have read before. Once they have worked through a text, rereading comes easier and can greatly improve rate and prosody.

Table 3.4

Method	Neurological Impress Method	Echo Reading	Repeated Reading	Readers' Theater
Description	Reading with student.	Reading before student. Students echo sentence by sentence.	Students reread text.	Students read and perform script of text.

Vocabulary

Focusing on teaching new words to readers as a tutor can be overwhelming at times. There is no way to teach every word in a new text. Within the tutoring sessions, there are two ways we will teach vocabulary: implicitly and explicitly. Readers will learn new words implicitly using the context and ideas in the text you are reading to them. This can also be done when they are reading themselves. Exposing students to new vocabulary words allows them to learn some of the new words as they understand the text. There are times when some vocabulary words should be explicitly taught in isolation. Identifying words that students should be taught before or as they read can assist them in not only reading the word but also in using the spelling patterns within the word to learn how words work. Teaching specific words can be done by discussion, concept maps, or direct instruction using word study. Using discussion as a teaching method involves introducing the new word and using the text to bring readers into an understanding of the word based on their background knowledge and knowledge they pull from the text. Concept maps can assist readers by connecting the meaning of the word to examples and non-examples. This method should be used for words common enough for students to encounter in future readings. Word study will be detailed in a later section. A few of the ways to teach vocabulary that will be used in tutoring are listed in Table 3.5.

Table 3.5

Method	Indirect Methods			Direct Methods	
	Wide Reading	Word Consciousness	Maintain High Quality Oral Language	Concept Map	Using Context
Description	Reading aloud to students and allowing students to read a wide variety of texts exposes them to new vocabulary in context.	Model and promote an interest and awareness of words as students talk and read with you (Scott & Nagy, 2004).	Model high quality oral language as you interact with students.	Concept maps use synonyms and antonyms as examples, guiding students through the words they are learning.	Assisting students as they read to understand new vocabulary using the context in the text. (NRP, 2003)

Phonemic Awareness

Knowing that phonemic awareness is the knowledge about how sounds in language can be segmented and manipulated, teaching readers about phonemic awareness is auditory as well. The most common method of teaching about sounds is reading and singing rhymes. Readers can begin to distinguish between rhyming and non-rhyming words by hearing them sung or read. Other language activities can model how to segment words and blend them orally.

Table 3.6

Phonemic Awareness Activity	
Segment	Have students segment sounds. You can use sound boxes or Elkonin boxes for this activity as well. Map — /m/ /a/ /p/ Much — /m/ /u/ /ch/
Blending	Write the word on a dry erase board and have students use their finger to draw a line under the word as they put the sounds together. /m/ /a/ /p/ ———— → /m/ /u/ /ch/ ———— →
Isolating and deleting	Have students isolate a specific sound in a word. Ask students to identify the beginning, middle, or ending sound of a word: What's the beginning (middle or ending) sound of "bunt?" For deletion have the students delete the ending sound of "bunt" → to make "bun."

Phonics

Phonics instruction spans at least five approaches, and for our purposes we will rely on spelling through phonics and embedded phonics. Spelling through phonics relies on having students use invented spelling to learn what sounds each letter makes. Since reading and writing letters using their sounds are closely connected (Adams, 1990), having students write to learn about sounds can be beneficial for their reading. Spelling instruction is then focused on allowing students to learn letters by using their sounds as they write and then reading back their own writing. Embedded phonics teaches readers key letters and sounds

Table 3.7

Method	Synthetic Phonics	Analytic Phonics	Phonics Through Spelling	Phonics in Context	Analogy Phonics
Description	Convert letters into phonemes, and then blend the phonemes to form words (/c/a/t/= cat).	Analyze letter-sound relations once the word is identified (pat, push, park, pen).	Transform sounds into letters to write words.	Embedded with actual text—use sound-letter correspondences along with context cues to identify unfamiliar words.	Use parts of already known written words to identify new words.

(NRP, 2003)

based on the texts they are reading. If a reader is struggling with the short /a/ sound, he or she can read *The Cat in the Hat* with a focus on all the words that have a short /a/ sound. These phonics-based instructional methods can be easily built into the tutoring sessions and connected to reading and writing activities.

Word Study

Teaching word study is complex and goes from letter and sound instruction, as cited in the previous phonics section, to detailed instruction of spelling patterns, syllables, and word meanings. While word study is an important instructional tool, in tutoring sessions the time is limited and word study is meant to supplement the reading and writing activities. Many programs offer ways to teach about words, and two of the most common are Words Their Way (Bear, Invernizzi, Templeton, & Johnston, 2016) and Making Words (Cunningham, Hall, & Heggie, 2001). These programs provide you with games, and puzzles for readers to use as they deconstruct and build words.

Writing

Pedagogical content knowledge as it relates to writing is closely connected to certain types of writing. Recognizing that each stage in the process of writing is always a part of teaching writing, we emphasize the instructional methods related to how to assist students as they work through each phase. Beginning with prewriting, students need to know what type of writing is expected and then be provided with examples of the genre. Allowing them to discuss and read the expected type of writing is crucial before asking them to write a draft. Once prewriting has been completed, students should then be encouraged to draft their ideas. Drafting is a time for you to encourage their ideas without overemphasizing spelling and conventions. Once a draft is complete, then you may begin to assist the student in rereading his or her work to determine what the student can rearrange, add, delete, or change as far as the ideas in the piece. Finally, you move the student into polishing and editing word by word as the learner prepares to publish his or her work. Publishing can take the form of digital stories, handwritten or typed books, etc.

Summary

Understanding the basic areas of reading and writing, and the various ways to teach each area, is key as you begin to think about tutoring. This overview should give you an idea on how reading can be broken down into manageable skills and strategies to teach readers how to read. Each area is much more complex than space allows, but as you move into the following chapters you will see how to implement the ideas presented earlier in more detail to assist your planning and teaching. Please review your initial responses to the pre-reading questions and revise your answers.

Pre-Reading Questions

How can you use your content knowledge to tutor?

Evaluate your understanding of the content and pedagogical content knowledge you need to successfully tutor. List your strengths and areas in which you need more support.

What pedagogical content knowledge can you use as you plan lessons?

Chapter 4: What Do You Need to Know to Teach and Assess Literacy?

Curricular and Assessment Knowledge

What do you need to know about choosing materials and assessments as you tutor? Think about what you read as you were learning to read. Did you learn to read using children's books? Or through the use of basal readers or textbooks? There are many instructional materials and entire programs designed to teach reading. Each one is unique and guided by its own theory and ideas on how young learners learn to read. Maybe you do not remember how you learned to read. That is common for many of us, but you may remember what you read at an early age. Depending on the trends and educational policies of the time when you were taught to read, you probably had some type of reading program. You may remember reading in small groups with your teacher where all of you had the same book. The books you read may have been little books with short stories or big heavy anthologies full of short stories or parts of stories. Some reading instruction relied on story kits in which you moved up levels by color as you read and answered questions after every story. You may have read stories or short passages on the computer and answered multiple-choice questions for points and rewards. Each of these types of programs have their pros and cons and shape how reading instruction is conducted. For our purposes in the tutoring program, we will focus not on one specific preset program with a script and set order of books, but on a developmental view of reading that encourages the use of leveled readers, rich literature, and informational texts set at specific reading levels. One reason for this is the need to carefully select texts for struggling readers that are accessible and meet their needs rather than a set program that may not support their growth. To find the correct books and materials, ongoing assessment is key.

There are many types of reading and writing assessments. You have probably taken a multiple-choice test at some point in your schooling. Do you remember reading paragraphs or words and having to fill in a bubble to indicate your answer? Standardized tests are one way to assess reading, but in our tutoring program, we center our assessments on observing readers and writers and using specific observational checklists and inventories to learn exactly what they know beyond filling in a bubble. While multiple-choice tests for reading can show us something about how readers understand a text, especially when compared with other readers, we also know they can guess at answers and that we cannot always tell why they did well or did not do well. Therefore, we choose to use more authentic methods to determine how well readers are doing as they read various types of texts.

Purpose of the Chapter

The purpose of this chapter is to describe the various types of curricular materials and assessments that are available as you plan your sessions. We emphasize the use of materials and assessments that are engaging and allow students to demonstrate their knowledge in the most natural ways possible. While we will cover quite a few assessments, the most beneficial way to understand your student's progress is to closely observe and take notes during and after each session as you notice the ways in which your learner is understanding and engaging in the activities. Before you read this chapter, please take a moment to answer the pre-reading questions that follow. Record your answers so when you are done reading you can go back and review what you have learned.

Pre-Reading Questions

How would you select materials to teach reading and writing?
How would you select assessments to evaluate your student?

The following key terms will be covered in this chapter.

Key Terms

Curricular Materials

This term will help as you begin to think about the materials you will select for your student. Knowing what is available and how to use it will make your sessions work well for both you and your student. All of these are commonly used in schools and other tutoring programs.

What Do I Need to Know About Literacy Curricular Materials?

It is crucial to be aware of and understand the various teaching materials available for tutoring. Choosing the wrong text can make struggling readers discouraged and set them back in their learning; on the other hand, using books that are too easy will not allow them to learn and improve their abilities. Different texts have different purposes and features that make them easier or more difficult, and determining which types to use with your reader at various points in his or her development is key to assisting the learner during tutoring sessions.

Knowing the basic areas of literacy and how to teach them is very closely tied to the materials you use in your instruction. Most students can be somewhat successful with the books and supplementary materials purchased by the district or school. But for struggling readers, some materials may not be appropriate. In the following segments, we define and provide examples of the most commonly used reading materials with brief suggestions for their use.

Curricular Materials

Curricular materials include any type of programs or materials used during instruction.

Curricular Materials: Types of Texts

In reading instruction, curricular materials typically include various types of text, mostly in the form of books, but technology can bring digital texts into instruction as well. There are various ways that books can be written for instruction. Of course, there are always the popular children's literature books many of us know and love to read, but at times these books can be difficult for beginning and struggling readers. Therefore, publishers and researchers decades ago began creating books specifically meant for teaching reading (Smith, 2002/1934). There are several ways to control the difficulty of a book (Clay, 1991). We will focus on the following:

- Word frequency
- Vocabulary
- Predictability

Word frequency simply refers to the amount of times words are repeated in a book. The more times readers see a word, the more likely they will remember and learn it. This is not true for all readers, but it is one way to make a text more readable. Vocabulary is tied to the type of words included in a text. As a reader yourself, you know that some words are easier than others. If readers are unfamiliar with words due to their background knowledge and/or they are faced with words that are complex and contain many syllables, they will find the text difficult. Predictability is related to both text predictability and predictability between the text and the illustrations or pictures. Predictable text is text that is repetitive and provides the reader with repeated patterns. These patterns allow readers to rely on memory as they learn to read. Another way text can be predictable is to match up closely with any pictures or illustrations. Beginning and struggling readers rely on pictures to help them as they learn to read. The following chart provides an overview of each type of text and its purposes.

Table 4.1

Text	Purpose	Features	Format
Basal Readers	Graded levels of difficulty by grade levels	Grade-level focus. Mixture of literature, informational text, controlled vocabulary	Anthologies of literature Small, group text sets
Leveled Readers	Graded levels of difficulty by text features	Predictable text and illustrations	Small, sequentially leveled individual books
Decodable Text	Graded levels of difficulty by phonic elements	Specifically highlight certain spelling patterns using repetition	Small, brief individual books
Literature (Narrative/ Fiction)	Enjoyment	Varies according to genre	Varies according to genre
Informational (Nonfiction)	Inform	Varies according to purpose Academic language and vocabulary	Varies according to purpose

Basal Readers

Basal readers are typically published by large publishing companies that provide books and teacher instructional manuals for entire schools by grade level. Each grade level receives a classroom set of books considered to be at that particular grade's reading level. The large basal reader text collections are rarely used in tutoring programs, but it is important to understand these materials since many students are reading them in their classrooms. The books are sometimes supplemented by other texts very similar to leveled readers to account for those students who are not reading at grade level. These books are usually shorter and introduce fewer new words with less complexity than the grade-level books.

Leveled Readers

Leveled readers are carefully constructed to reading levels more discrete than those leveled by grade. Each book slowly becomes more difficult through the text features of word frequency, vocabulary, and predictability. By making each level more difficult in smaller increments than basal grade-level spans, the leveled readers provide a slower progression of difficulty and make instruction easier to pinpoint. These are commonly used in tutoring programs and are leveled by numbers or letters that correlate with developmental reading levels and grade levels.

Decodable Texts

Decodable texts are effective for working with readers who need to learn to focus on sounding out words. The assumption behind creating books that rely on certain phonic elements is that readers will learn to rely on decoding each word as they read. Meaning becomes secondary in these books as the goal of using and repeating specific sounds is critical. These texts are easily identified by their text patterns, (e.g., "a cat sat on a mat").

All of these levels can be connected by using a conversion chart. Many publishers of materials have created charts so teachers will know how to level the books they are selecting. A quick search online will present you with several options and charts to show you where your book's level falls. Most charts begin with kindergarten, go to eighth grade, and will include the following:

Table 4.2

Developmental Reading Level	Grade Level	Basal Level	Fountas and Pinnell-Leveled Readers	Lexile
Emergent	Kindergarten	Readiness	A	Begins at upper grades

Subsequent rows will address fluent readers who read at an eighth-grade level. Each row details the developmental reading level, the grade level, and continues across to include leveled readers and Lexile levels.

Lexile Levels

Lexile levels have come into prominence recently (https://lexile.com/about-lexile/lexile-overview/lexile-infographic/). The Lexile framework uses Lexile numbers to level all types of books and is now a large part of many school district and testing leveling systems. See Chapter 7 for more information.

Literature (narrative/fiction)

Children's literature is not written for instructional purposes, yet it can be used in reading instruction. Children's books are engaging, have complex and interesting stories, and do not seek to control vocabulary and phonic elements. While these aspects can make the text more difficult for struggling readers, they also bring motivation and interest into reading. Planning instruction with children's literature is possible and many books are now leveled in ways that correlate with grade level and leveled reader systems. See Chapter 5 for more details.

Informational Texts (nonfiction)

Just as children's literature is not specifically written for instruction, many nonfiction or informational texts are not specifically designed to teach reading. They may vary in the features of text and be somewhat difficult to level. With careful instruction, however, they can be used effectively and should be a part of tutoring. Many students find the nonfiction topics to be interesting and compelling reading, which encourages them to read. Many publishers level books using grade or Lexile levels. A quick Internet search of titles or levels will help you find books by level.

Types of Writing Materials

Writing instruction does not have to depend on any type of particular program, but there are many supporting resources available for writing instruction. Some materials detail how to set up a classroom writing workshop for all students to write independently (Atwell, 2014; Calkins, 1994), while others explain and illustrate how to do specific writing tasks using prompts, checklists, and rubrics (Calkins). Both types of supporting materials can be helpful and provide guidelines and ideas for instruction. The downfall of some writing curricular materials is their misuse as worksheets in which students simply fill in blanks. As a tutor, you want to focus on using many different writing ideas that relate to the reading activities you are teaching.

Types of Word Study Materials

Word study is the examination of the ways words are spelled based on their spelling patterns and meanings (Williams, Phillips-Birdsong, Hufnagel, Hungler, & Lundstrom, 2009). Many types of materials have been created to teach about words, and there are very specific programs that begin with activities at the kindergarten level of understanding the individual sounds each letter makes all the way to complex spelling patterns such as *–tion*. Along with these prescripted programs, there are many materials that can be used to teach about words, such as apps, magnetic letters, dry erase boards, and simply pen and paper.

Assessment

The key to effective instruction is ongoing assessment. While assessment will be included throughout the text and added into each tutoring session, there are a few key components to understand before you tutor. The following sections will define the basic areas of reading and writing assessment.

What Assessment Knowledge Do I Need to Evaluate Readers?

Reading assessments are designed to determine overall reading levels. Our tutoring program relies on informal assessments, which are designed to be used in your tutoring sessions. All of the assessments described in this section are focused on observing readers as they engage in reading- and writing-related tasks; they are not formal assessments such as standardized tests.

Anecdotal Notes

Taking notes as you teach is the most important way to assess your student. Anecdotal notes merely mean that you try to take notes on specific behaviors or comments your student makes as he or she is actually reading and writing. These notes can assist you as you plan your next lesson and over time can help you determine what patterns you are seeing. For instance, if you notice your reader becomes lost while reading and skips lines of text, you may want to work on providing the learner with a pointer or card to help the student keep his or her place in the text. If they sound out words as they write, you will want to note that as well. These types of observations help you to record how your students are reading and writing and provide you with ideas on how to help them. Most structured assessments have very specific items to record, and keeping open anecdotal notes allows for more observations and ways to see how your student is doing day to day.

Informal Reading Inventories

Informal reading inventories (IRI) are comprehensive reading assessments tested and designed to evaluate readers' accuracy, comprehension, and fluency (Paris & Carpenter, 2003). There are many IRIs available with different focuses (Nilsson, 2008) such as grade level and types of test, but overall they all contain the same following components: (1) word recognition/accuracy, fluency, and (3) comprehension. Most IRIs include text passages, comprehension questions and activities (prediction, retelling, main idea), and fluency measure so the assessor is able to complete all areas easily and score the student's reading within the forms. IRIs provide a reading level for the reader based on all of the areas analyzed holistically. They come in sets for you to administer and scoring is provided with clear calculations for you.

Running Records

Running records (also a part of IRIs) are a written record of oral reading and measure word recognition, sometimes called accuracy. The assessor has a copy of the text or a blank page and records every error or miscue the student makes as he or she reads. This includes writing down words read incorrectly, words added into the text, and noting words not read. These records are a part of regular instruction and allow us to analyze the types of reading mistakes or miscues the reader is making for future planning.

Miscue Analysis

Miscue analysis utilizes the information gathered in the running record to analyze the reader's miscues. Miscues refer to the mistakes readers make in relation to the three basic cueing systems referred to in Chapter 2. Psycholinguistic theory views reading as a combination of meaning, syntax, and visual/graphophonic information that readers rely on as they process text (Clay, 1991; Goodman, 1967). Therefore, in assessing readers, we can use their miscues as recorded in running records to analyze the reading cueing systems they are relying on most, using, and avoiding. Miscues are categorized by their relationship to how students are using meaning, syntax or grammar, and visual information such as sounding out words or using pictures. For example, if your students use primarily visual cues, then you will see this in your running record miscue analysis.

Comprehension Assessments

Comprehension is complex and there are many ways to assess comprehension. For our purposes, we focus on the three types of comprehension (literal, inferential, and critical) and their assessment at three stages of reading, (before, during, and after). While comprehension can be assessed using writing activities, drawing, and discussion, we highlight the use of asking students questions as a means of learning about their understanding of what they are reading. Asking students to predict what the text will be about before they read is a common way to check on how much they know about the topic. At times, if students have a significant amount of knowledge about a new text, they may bring that knowledge to the comprehension questions without having to really understand the text. Asking them what they know before they read gives us an idea of what they already know and how it compares to what they will learn by reading. Questioning the student about the text during reading can help you assess his or her ongoing comprehension. Finally, asking questions at the end of reading allows for evaluating a student's comprehension of the entire text including larger themes and ideas along with details and key points. There are many comprehension checklists you can use to monitor strategy use, prepared comprehension questions to analyze their skill in answering different types of questions, or you may create your own questions to assess how well they understood the text.

Fluency Assessments

Fluency is assessed in two ways (Guszak, 1992; Kuhn et al., 2010). Rate is used to determine how many words students read per minute. Taking a rate of reading is easy and can be done by taking a 15-second timing as the student reads, and then counting the number of words read and multiplying by four. Or for more fluent readers, time their oral reading for one minute and count the number of words read correctly (words correct per minute, or wcpm). Both of these methods provide you with a clear number of words read per minute. To be sure of a student's rate, you need to take several rates. Using the Oral Reading Fluency Norms chart developed by Hasbrouck and Tindal (2005), you can see where your student's fluency rate falls for his or her grade level. Another way to assess fluency is qualitatively. To assess qualitative fluency, listen as the student reads, and describe the reading according to expression, or prosody, using key terms. Slow, choppy word-by-word reading versus smooth reading of phrases with correct expression and intonation are typical descriptors of reading fluency. Both of these areas together demonstrate measures of a student's fluency. There are also several assessments that provide a leveled text excerpt and take fluency ratings, typically called fluency probes. Of course, comprehending the text is also an important component of fluency. A fluent reader is able to read accurately (automaticity), quickly, and with expression while understanding what is read.

Overall, reading assessments evaluate accuracy, comprehension, and fluency. Once you know the basic materials and methods for teaching reading, you can begin to select appropriate books that are both interesting and readable for your student. Reading can be difficult so learning how to evaluate books and match them well with readers can make a big difference in their learning and enjoyment.

Writing Assessments

Assessing writing involves close observation (e.g., anecdotal notes) and specific rubrics and checklists that monitor how students are using the writing process and how they are meeting the expectations of the particular types or genre of writing they are composing. There are various books that have useful checklists and rubrics to use as guides to evaluate the writing process and genre selection. There are also writing continuums and rubrics that can be used to assist you in observing students' writing and in evaluating their final work products (Calkins, 2014).

Word/Spelling Assessments

Spelling assessments evaluate word knowledge from letter and sound relationships (c-a-t-) to the more complex spelling patterns such as bl-, gh, etc. Some assessments ask students to spell particular words to learn what letters and spelling patterns they can produce (Bear et al., 2016) while other assessments ask students to identify letters and their sounds by reading them (Clay, 1985). Collecting and analyzing students' running records and their writing samples can also provide information on how they use their knowledge of letters and sounds as they actually read and write.

Summary

Understanding how books are designed and how they are used to assist readers in learning and using specific strategies as they read is key to successful tutoring. Choosing texts is the most important part of tutoring. The wrong book can frustrate readers while the correct book can move them slowly forward. With experience and careful analysis, you can gradually move your student up levels with key supporting texts and instruction. Do not hesitate to abandon a book that is not working for your student. It often takes time to find the types of texts that motivate a reluctant reader. Rachel tutored a student who enjoys working with robotics, but she did not know this even though she had administered an interest inventory, had multiple conversations with the student about topics that interest him, and selected a variety of texts and genres for him to read. It was serendipitous that she found a leveled reader about robots. The book examined the many uses of robots and robotics in society today. Rachel found that her student, a struggling fifth-grade reader, had a robust background knowledge about robots and robotics. She was able to find other texts about robots—fiction and nonfiction at varying reading levels—that she used during tutoring sessions. Using these books she was able to create word walls, develop writing activities, and teach reading strategies that have benefitted the student. While text selection is important, carefully observing a student's writing can also allow you to see how he or she is progressing over time. Please review your initial answers and revise them as needed.

Pre-Reading Questions

How can you use your curricular knowledge to tutor?

Assessments should inform your instruction. Analyze your student's informal reading inventory, spelling inventory, and writing samples. What patterns do you notice across all three assessments? How will you use this information to plan your next few lessons?

What assessments can you use as you plan lessons?

PART III: READING TUTORING COMPONENTS AND LESSON PLANS

The third section focuses on reading instruction and how to plan and implement each part of the tutoring program. Each chapter covers a specific type of instruction, explains its purpose, and ties it to teaching English learners, followed by sample lesson plans for beginning, intermediate, and advanced tutors. Chapter 5 examines read alouds and shared reading, Chapter 6 covers guided reading, and Chapter 7 describes independent reading lessons.

Chapter 5: Teaching Reading
Read Alouds and Shared Reading

Do you remember being read to? Do you remember the sounds of the words as a parent, teacher or caregiver read aloud from a colorful picture book filled with rhyming words or repetitive phrases? Rachel remembers watching a group of young children sitting on the carpet crisscross applesauce with hands folded in laps and eyes focused on the big book version of Audrey Wood's *The Napping House* (Wood & Wood, 2009), enjoying the rhythm of their teacher's voice as she read aloud to them. She observed their faces as

they sat enthralled while led page by page through the story, hypnotized by the teacher's melodic voice that punctuated the cumulative process of the text. She saw their little bodies tense as each animal piled onto the bed on top of granny and the little child, prompting several children to pull their hands from their lap and place them on the sides of their face as they began to anticipated what would happen next. As the story reaches the part where the flea bites the mouse, the students know their predictions are coming true and with excitement they inch ever nearer the front to get as close to the story as possible. By the end of the story, no one in the "Napping House" is sleeping and the children, definitely awake as well, don't want the story to end. The teacher reassures them they will cover the story the next day during shared reading, or they can review the book during literacy centers or during their independent reading time. The read aloud is central to this teacher's literacy instruction and will set the stage for many other literacy events that will occur throughout the day. As a tutor, you will need to understand how read alouds, shared reading and writing, independent reading and writing, and guided reading and writing are all important components of literacy instruction.

This chapter is designed to explore the definition of literacy as it relates to the notion of how readers can "read their world" and ultimately "read the word" (Freire, 1970; Freire & Macedo, 1987). In reading their world, students need to come to an understanding about the world or context within the text before they can begin to read the word or understand the words within the text. Therefore, reading the world and reading the word are permanently bound together; you cannot have a true literacy experience without both. In other words, you may have students who can word call or read the words beautifully, but not have a true understanding of what they read because they do not have an understanding of the world or context the text describes (Freire & Macedo, 1987; Gee, 2015). Reading aloud to students is one way to expand their existing worlds. As an example, let's look at the world or domain of science. Students working on a lab assignment could be asked to measure liquids in a buret to a certain level and then draw off a certain amount of liquid. Students without an understanding of what the word "draw" means in science could mistakenly think they needed to draw a picture of the buret and not actually release a certain amount of liquid from it. There are many examples of words students can read but not understand because they have a different meaning in a different domain or "world." In the tutoring program, students will be exposed to a variety of text genres and multimodal literacy practices to introduce them to, and expand their understanding of, new "worlds" or domains. To share new worlds and reinforce concepts of known worlds, you should employ a variety of literacy instructional practices such as read alouds, shared reading and writing, independent and guided reading, and writing throughout each session.

Before you read this chapter, please take a moment to answer the pre-reading questions that follow. Record your answers so when you are done reading you can go back and review what you have learned.

Purpose of the Chapter

Pre-Reading Questions

What do you know about the importance of read alouds?
What do you know about the key components of literacy instruction?
The following terms are important to understand since they will be used throughout tutoring.

Key Terms

Read Aloud   Interactive Read Aloud   Genres

Understanding how each of these terms apply to tutoring and literacy practices is essential in helping tutored students improve their reading and writing. During tutoring, you will engage your student in a variety of literacy practices that include reading books aloud.

What Are Read Alouds?

A read aloud is an excellent opportunity to share a book or a section of a book that you read aloud as your student listens and interacts with the text. There are many reasons to read aloud to your student and we will discuss those reasons in depth in the section on "Why read alouds are important." A read aloud is not just a matter of grabbing a book off a shelf and reading it to a child. A read aloud takes time and planning.

> **Read Aloud**
>
> A read aloud is an excellent opportunity to model reading aloud with expression and intonation to your student.

In the beginning of tutoring you should give students an interest survey or inventory to gather more information about them. This simple inventory is just one way to gather information to select appropriate text for the student by learning the types of books, genres, and activities he or she may be interested in and enjoys. Knowing the student's interest is a great place to start in selecting a read aloud text. For example, if you know a student is interested in being a police officer when he or she grows up and also likes dogs, you might read aloud the Caldecott medal winner, *Office Buckle and Gloria*, by Peggy Rathman (1995). This humorous and delightful story tells the unique relationship between a police officer and a police dog named Gloria. Or if you have a student who loves baseball you might read Jonah Winter's (2008) *Roberto Clemente: Pride of the Pittsburgh Pirates*, beautifully illustrated by Raúl Colón. If a student enjoys music you might read Monica Brown's (2013) *Tito Puente Mambo King, Rey del Mambo,* or the Coretta Scott King award winner, *Trombone Shorty,* written by Troy Andrew (2015) with stunning illustrations by

Bryan Collier. Or perhaps you could read Robert Levine's (2000) informational text, *The Story of the Orchestra*, so students can learn more about musical instruments and famous composers. Sometimes you can pick a book to read aloud because you want to share rich and rhythmic language with the student. Sometimes you can read a text that may be challenging for the student to read independently or without instructional support. There are many wonderful books to read to model the musicality of language but one of my favorite books is Tony DiTerlizzi's (2002) Caldecott honor book, *The Spider and the Fly*. There are many texts and genres to choose from for a read aloud. First, decide the purpose or why you are reading aloud. If you are using read aloud to teach very specific strategies or concepts such as to teach vocabulary, comprehension strategies, or literary elements, an interactive read aloud might be the best method to use. More information on interactive read alouds is provided in this chapter. It is important to have a purpose for reading aloud to your student. As such, before finding that great book, get to know your student, set a purpose for the read aloud, and then find a text to read aloud. Once you have decided your purpose and selected a text to read to your student, you should practice reading the book. Read the book silently to yourself first so you understand the story and the characters or information. Then read the book a second time aloud to practice using appropriate intonation, inflection, and modulation. Your voice should help the story come alive and captivate your audience. You can practice reading a book aloud several times so you feel comfortable reading it to your student. Remember, a read aloud does not have to be a storybook; it can also be an informational text or a chapter from a longer young adult novel. Select a few strategic places to stop to discuss certain aspects of the story. Do not spend too much time talking through the text, as this will disrupt the flow of the story. You can use an interactive read aloud to spend more time discussing a text and inviting student response. A read aloud is an important literacy practice that you will engage in every tutoring session.

For an example of a read aloud please view the video.

Video 5.1

The basic essential elements of a read aloud are listed in the following section.

Essential Elements of a Read Aloud

1.   Set a purpose for the read aloud.

2.   Know your student's interests (student interest inventory) and reading level (prior assessments) to assist you in selecting a text.

3. Practice reading the book silently and aloud before reading the book to your student.

4. Strategically select a few stopping points throughout the text (no more than three or four depending on book length and purpose of the read aloud).

5. Read with clarity and intonation, stopping at the preselected pages (mark these pages with Sticky Notes).

These elements cover the basic steps to prepare and read the text to your student.

Why Are Read Alouds Important?

As teachers, we know the act of reading aloud to children is beneficial and an important part of good literacy practice. As we read aloud to our students we listen to their responses, the comments they make about the text, the higher-order processing that occurs, and the connections they make to the text, their world, and the world around them. We hear them mimic our voices and intonation when they reread the text on their own and use vocabulary they learned from the text as well. We see and understand the instructional practice that read alouds provide, but more than that we know there is research to support this practice. In 1985, the Report on the Commission on Reading stated, "The

single most important activity for building the knowledge required for eventual success in reading is reading aloud to children" (Anderson, Hiebert, Scott, & Wilkinson, 1985, p. 23). Furthermore, the report goes on to state, "The benefits are greatest when the child is an active participant, engaging in discussions about stories, learning to identify letters and words, and talking about the meanings of words." More than a decade later, in 1998, the National Research Council also highlighted the use of read alouds to support literacy instruction and recommended and promoted "adult-child shared book readings that stimulate verbal interactions" as a method of promoting literacy development (Snow, Burns, & Griffin, 1998, p 52). Since then researchers have looked at different aspects of literacy instruction through read alouds. Read alouds can also be used to help students with comprehension skills.

Listening Comprehension

Read alouds can help build listening comprehension skills (Morrow & Gambrell, 2002). Students may not be able to read the text on their own but they understand the content from the read aloud book and can contribute to the conversations and dialogue surrounding the text. By reading aloud a text that might be just out of a student's reading ability, but one in which the student has background knowledge, the learner can contribute personal thoughts, ideas, and connections and show his or her knowledge of the subject matter. Read alouds can also help a student build and expand their vocabulary (Neuman & Dwyer, 2011).

Expand and Introduce New Vocabulary

Another one of Rachel's favorite books to read aloud to young children is *Click, Clack, Moo: Cows that Type* by Doreen Cronin (2000). While most of the text is filled with sight words and decodable text, this book has a few challenging words that are fun to explore with children such as the word "strike"—the cows and hens go on strike and do not produce milk or eggs. Another word is "furious." Farmer Brown is furious that his farm animals are going on strike. The picture cues are excellent in depicting a very angry farmer. Finally, two other great words in the book are "neutral "and "ultimatum." Duck, who is not involved in the strike, is a "neutral party" in the situation so he is charged with delivering the ultimatum or demand to the farmer. Children are involved in a wonderful read aloud that is teaching them not only comprehension listening skills, but also new and challenging vocabulary. This book is just one of many that can be used to teach new vocabulary to children. Besides teaching vocabulary, read alouds can also provide models for how the English language works. Teaching syntactic development is good for all children but especially English learners (ELs) who are learning English as a new language and figuring out how this new language is structured.

Syntactic Development

By listening to read alouds, young children, adolescent readers, and ELs can listen to how the English language works. Just as we discussed in Chapter 2, we respect students' home languages and dialects, but we also want to familiarize them with various language patterns. Reading aloud is an excellent way to accomplish this because they are able to hear you read complex text. *Voices in the Park* by Anthony Browne (2001) is a great book to show how the English language is rich in descriptive adjectives. This book is told by four voices; the characters are in the park at the same time but each tells of their singular experience at the park. By listening to this story, students can hear how the English language comes together in a creative format. Reading aloud to students can also motivate and encourage them to read.

Motivation

The rich storytelling of narrative stories, the fun rhyming words of poetry, or the descriptive information from nonfiction can be a motivating factor that ignites a student's desire to pick up a book and read. Students may be intimidated by a text's length, vocabulary, or content until they have heard it read aloud and realize the book is within their reading ability. Whether students pretend-read the text or read it conventionally, a read aloud gives them the opportunity to hear the words and understand the story so they might be more willing to read the text on their own. In addition to motivating students to read the text, read alouds provide students with the opportunity to hear the reader use intonation, inflection, and pace. Prosodic reading allows students to hear the rhythmic sounds of the English language and the structure of different genres used in books.

Genres/Text Types

Selecting a variety of genres to read aloud to your students will introduce them to different text formats, vocabulary, and content.

Genre

Genre means type or kind. In children's literature, genre refers to the specific type of text selected such as a picture book, realistic fiction, historical fiction, fantasy, poetry, traditional literature, or nonfiction.

While reading fantasy and poetry can be fun and engaging for students, reading realistic fiction could help students make concrete connections to the characters and issues they may be going through. *Enemy Pie*, by Derek Munson (2000), is a delightful and insightful realistic fiction book to help children learn how to get along with the very people who bother and bully them in school. Another genre that helps children understand themselves and the past is historical fiction, which can introduce new vocabulary and concepts and make links to and expand on social science concepts. Reading traditional literature, stories passed down orally throughout centuries and cultures, shows students how we are more alike than different as they hear about fairy tales, myths, legends, and folktales from around the world. Reading biographies is an exciting way to introduce students to famous people who have had an influence on the country through sports, politics, the arts, government, and social justice. Finally, introducing informational text in a read aloud can help students develop an understanding of text structures such as headings, subheading, graphs, charts, diagrams, and captions. By reading nonfiction texts to students, especially ELs, academic vocabulary can be introduced, highlighted, and defined in context. Informational text is also written using very different text structures from fiction texts. Pointing out the text structures found in nonfiction such as headings, subheadings, captions, graphics, and charts to show students how they can glean information from these structures to help them understand the content is important. Another method to help your student understand text or make connections to text is through visualizations.

Visualization

Once you have practiced reading the book aloud several times, go back into the story and think about places in the text where you can stop and ask the student to visualize the story. Ask your student to think of the story as a movie in his or her mind as you read aloud (Layne, 2015). You can stop at certain points within the story and ask your student to describe what he or she sees as you read the text aloud. While visualization is a fun activity that most students enjoy, it is also an excellent comprehension strategy (Tompkins, 2013). Visualization is also important for English learners (ELs). Providing ELs with the opportunity to see images of the text read in their head and talk about what they see can help them better comprehend the text, and can help you gauge what the student knows and understands. To help ELs understand how visualization works, read a short section of text and guide them through the visualization process by telling them to "see" like a movie in their mind what you describe based on the text. Model the process by telling them what you see as you read the text. To initiate more active participation in the read aloud process, you might want to engage in an interactive read aloud.

Interactive Read Aloud

An interactive read aloud invites active student participation and interaction. In an interactive read aloud you are purposefully selecting activities or strategies to teach throughout the read aloud process, such as specific vocabulary to discuss and highlight, or the author's voice, sentence fluency, or the use of metaphor or other literary elements. For ELs (and other students as well), you might foreground the vocabulary prior to reading the text and assist them in making connections to the words and their meaning. You can invite your student to make personal connections or use personal descriptions of the vocabulary words (for example, if the word you are discussing from the story describes puppies as "frisky," students may talk about their dogs as being playful or frisky too). (Price & Bradley, 2016).

> **Interactive Read Aloud**
>
> An interactive read aloud involves active student participation and strategic instruction.

In addition, make sure you are asking appropriate questions depending on your student's needs, such as open-ended, close-ended, or clarifying questions and responding to students' questions and comments in an authentic way. The goal of an interactive read aloud is to engage students in active discourse, and thinking. Price and Bradley (2016) call it being "responsive, instead of directive" (p. 712). In other words, you are accepting and responding to students' comments, suggestions, and questions and making them aware their words and thoughts are valued.

As you plan for an interactive read aloud you once again need to know your student's interests, abilities (using your informal assessment information), and background knowledge. Before you begin, preview the text with your student. Next, check or activate their background knowledge about the content. Finally, decide on the strategies you want to reinforce, teach, or practice—such as fluency, story elements, structure, or comprehension. As you read and interact with students about the text, make sure to listen to their responses and comments closely. If your student seems confused or is providing feedback that doesn't correspond with the text, make sure to stop and correct any misconceptions and provide more support for the student. Interactive read alouds can be used for students of all ages.

For an example of an interactive reading activity, please view the video.

Video 5.2

Reading to Older Students

Interactive read alouds are not just for young children. There are many wonderful upper-level story picture books and informational texts that can be used to model reading complex text, or introduce challenging vocabulary and comprehension strategies. In addition, you can read a chapter book aloud to have the student visualize the characters, setting, plot, and other literary elements. Many of the same genres mentioned earlier can be used with older students—including science fiction and its subgenre, dystopian fiction (*Hunger Games*, etc.)—as interactive read alouds. Dystopian fiction has become very popular with adolescent readers. Using dystopian, science fiction, or graphic novels as interactive read alouds can help motivate and encourage older students to read more. Never feel your student is too old for a read aloud or shared reading experience.

Shared Reading

Shared reading is a literacy technique in which both the tutor and the student read the text together and the tutor provides supports throughout the reading to assist the student in tackling text using different modalities. In shared reading, the tutor provides strategic support before, during, and after the reading event. Shared reading is an opportunity to read *with* your student, unlike a read aloud where you are reading *to* your student. It is also an excellent way to provide different levels of support and to model a variety of reading skills and strategies tailored to your student's specific needs. The essential elements that follow will help you prepare for a shared reading lesson.

Essential Elements of Shared Reading

1. Decide on the instructional purpose for the shared reading.

2. Select a text that fits the instructional purpose and your student's interests (use different genres).

3. Read the text prior to sharing the text with the student (the text can be a text previously used as a read aloud).

4. Select no more than one or two strategies or skills to teach (or teaching points).

5. Find vocabulary or text features that may be challenging and prepare to discuss them prior to sharing the text.

6. Be prepared to model the reading process as you read with your student.

Knowing the steps involved in preparing for any reading activity is important. Preparation is the key to a successful tutoring experience for both you and your student. There are specific steps to implementing a read aloud and shared reading and those are discussed in more detail in the following section.

For an example of a shared reading activity, please view the video.

Video 5.3

Reading to or with English Learners

Reading aloud to all children, but especially to English learners, is an excellent method to model the multifaceted structure and flow of the English language. Reading aloud from a variety of genres will also benefit ELs as they learn how the English language works in narrative and informational text and how to access different academic registers (the way text is structured across content areas such as science, math, and social sciences). When reading to ELs in a read aloud format, the use of graphics, visuals, realia, and/or gestures can support their understanding of the vocabulary or concepts they will encounter within the text. Knowing your student's language proficiency will assist in text selection for the read aloud and shared reading experience. Purposefully select text with language understandable to the EL at his or her current level of English proficiency but one that will also provide some challenging text that can be taught through the read aloud or shared reading experience.

Reading Aloud Content Knowledge

Modeling reading aloud content knowledge is based on understanding the essential elements involved in the process of reading aloud.

1. Set your purpose for reading aloud.

2. Select different genres and texts in children's literature to read aloud.

3. Understanding how to model a read aloud.

4. Knowing where to pause to elicit student response in a read aloud.

Table 5.1 provides an overview of the areas covered in this section.

Table 5.1

Essential Elements	Description
Set your purpose for reading aloud	What is it you are trying to accomplish by reading the book aloud? Which behaviors are you modeling using the book selected?
Genre and text selection	Purposefully select a book for the read aloud. This selection should align with what your goal is for reading the book to your student.
Understanding how to model a read aloud	Pre-read the text. Practice reading the text aloud and practice elements you will teach or emphasize throughout the text.
Knowing where to pause or how to elicit student response	Know where and why you have paused in a certain place in the text. Listen to students' responses and follow up on their comments and questions. In other words, do not ignore what they have to say about the story.

Read aloud pedagogical content knowledge is focused on the ways reading aloud is taught.

Table 5.2 Read Aloud Pedagogical Content Knowledge

Essential Elements	Description
Set your purpose for reading aloud	Explain to the student the purpose for the read aloud.
Genre and text selection	Explain to the student why the text was selected.
Understanding how to model a read aloud	As you read aloud, listen to your voice or review your tape to see how you read the text (check for prosody, pacing, clarity).
Knowing where to pause or how to elicit student response	Know how you will engage the student in responding to questions.

Read aloud curricular knowledge is focused on the curricular materials associated with the read aloud.

Table 5.3 Read Aloud Curricular Knowledge

Essential Elements	Description
Set your purpose for reading aloud	School curricular materials (such as reading programs) will have an explicit purpose stated based on the read aloud lesson. Materials used for the following lessons below are based on children's literature and leveled texts selected to match student interest and lesson objectives.

Genre and text selection	School curricular materials often have stories written in specific genres that can be used for read aloud lessons. Materials used for the following lessons below are based on children's literature and leveled texts selected to match student interest and lesson objectives.
Understanding how to model a read aloud	School curricular materials may provide scant information on how to model a read aloud.
Knowing where to pause or how to elicit student response	School curricular materials may or may not provide stopping points or questions to use throughout the read aloud. For tutoring lessons, those will be based on strategy and skills taught based on student needs.

Planning for Read Alouds

Planning for read alouds depends on your purpose for selecting the text. Are you trying to model expressive reading, specific comprehension strategies, increase reading interest and motivation, or introduce different genres in children's literature? This section provides you with sample lesson plans at the beginning, intermediate, and advanced levels based on your understanding of read alouds. Each lesson sample and its accompanying template is designed to provide a framework for organizing your instruction.

Table 5.4 Beginner Lesson Plan: Read Alouds

Lesson Component	Purpose	Materials	Implementation		Observations/ Assessments
Read aloud 20 minutes	Select a purpose for the read aloud based on learning objectives, strategy, or modeling technique to be taught.	Picture book selected to model specific strategy and/or purpose.	Before reading	Have student make predictions based on the front cover. Provide comments to student's responses. Guide back to topic if needed. Provide plenty of wait time.	Observe how student attends to the text during read aloud. Listen to answers, predictions, questions, and comments made by the student.
			During reading	What do we know about …? Provide thought-provoking questions or comments to guide student through text.	
			After reading	Make connections to extend reading to self, other texts, or world.	

Table 5.5 Intermediate Lesson Plan: Read Aloud

Lesson Component	Purpose	Materials	Implementation		Observations/ Assessments
Read aloud 20 minutes	Select a purpose for the read aloud based on learning objectives, strategy, or modeling technique to be taught.	Picture book storybook (select from different genres: historical or realistic fiction)	Before reading	Use title to discuss: What do we know about …? Use title and picture on cover to discuss: What do you think is happening…? Ask "why" questions to elicit more details.	Observe how student attends to the text during read aloud. Listen to answers, predictions, questions, and comments from the student.
			During reading	Assist student in visualizing what could be happening in the story. Guide students in providing details.	
			After reading	Focus on story grammar to retell main ideas. Make more supporting comments, then ask questions.	

Shared Reading Content Knowledge

Modeling shared reading content knowledge is based on understanding the essential elements involved in the process of a shared reading.

1. Set your purpose for shared reading.

2. Select a text that fits the instructional purpose and your student's interests (use different genres).

3. Select strategies or skills to teach (or teaching points).

4. Model the reading process as you read with your student.

Table 5.6 Advanced Lesson Plan: Read Aloud

Lesson Component	Purpose	Materials	Implementation		Observations/ Assessments
Read aloud 20 minutes	Select a purpose for the read aloud based on learning objectives, strategy, or modeling technique to be taught.	Select an informational or nonfiction text.	Before reading	Introduce text with learning objectives as focus. Generate interest in the text. Make sure students understand text features. Preview the text if text structures are new to the students.	Observe how student attends to the text during read aloud. Listen to answers, predictions, questions, and comments from the student. Check retelling for clear understanding of the story structure elements.
			During reading	Create questions to ask during the read aloud that will meet objectives and purpose. Mark appropriate pages with Sticky Notes and questions. Follow up on student's comments.	
			After reading	Engage in activities that extend student's comprehension of the text: e.g., writing for a different purpose and from a different perspective. Use a sentence frame activity. Allow students to make connections to text. Ask student how story relates to him or her.	

Table 5.7 provides an overview of the areas covered in this section.

Table 5.7

Essential Elements	Description
Set your purpose for the shared reading	What is it you are trying to accomplish by reading the book together with the student? Which behaviors are you modeling using the book selected?
Text/genre selection	Purposefully select a book for the shared reading. This selection should align with what your goal is for reading the book with your student.
Select strategies or skills to teach	Decide upon the skills or strategy to teach during the shared reading.
Model the reading process as you read with your student	Carefully read the text with your student and model the reading process as you read (making meaning through reading).

Table 5.8 Shared reading pedagogical content knowledge is focused on the ways reading aloud is taught.

Table 5.8 Shared Reading Pedagogical Content Knowledge

Essential Elements	Description
Set your purpose for the shared reading	Explain to the student the purpose for the shared reading and introduce the text.
Text/genre selection	Explain to the student the type of text and why it was selected.
Select strategies or skills to teach	Teach one or two strategies or skills based on the lesson objective and purpose.
Model the reading process as you read with your student	Decide how the text will be shared: tutor reads alone the first time, tutor and student read together the second time, tutor fades in and out while providing support when needed for a third reading.

Read aloud curricular knowledge is focused on the curricular materials associated with the read aloud.

Planning for Shared Reading

Planning for shared reading depends on your purpose for selecting the text. Which teaching points will you highlight during the shared reading? This section provides you with

Table 5.9 Shared Reading Curricular Content Knowledge

Essential Elements	Description
Set your purpose for the shared reading	Materials used are based on texts selected to match student's interest, lesson objectives, and purpose.
Text/genre selection	Tutoring materials are selected based on the student's interest and literacy needs.
Select strategies or skills to teach	Use text to teach skills or strategies based on the student's interest and literacy needs.
Model the reading process as you read with your student	Curricular materials or selected text are used to model the reading process.

sample lesson plans at the beginning, intermediate, and advanced level based on your understanding of shared reading. Each lesson sample and its accompanying template is designed to provide you with a framework for organizing your instruction.

Table 5.10 Beginner Lesson Plan: Shared Reading

Lesson Component	Purpose	Materials	Implementation		Observations/ Assessments
Shared reading 10 minutes	Select a purpose for the shared reading based on learning objectives, strategy, or modeling technique to be taught (remember, you read with the student).	Select text (poetry) based on specific strategy and/or teaching points.	Before reading	Introduce text with learning objectives as focus.	Observe how student attends to the text during shared reading. Listen to how student participates.
			During reading	Focus on teaching points: punctuation, sentence structure, alliteration, etc.	
			After reading	Revisit the text or have student reread. Reinforce teaching points. Engage student in a discussion.	

Table 5.11 Intermediate Lesson Plan: Shared Reading

Lesson Component	Purpose	Materials	Implementation		Observations/ Assessments
Shared reading 10 minutes	Select a purpose for the shared reading based on learning objectives, strategy or modeling technique to be taught. (remember you read with the student)	Select text (short narrative) based on specific strategy and/or teaching points.	Before reading	Introduce text with learning objectives as focus. Have student make predictions based on front cover and title.	Observe how student attends to the text during shared reading. Listen to how student participates.
			During reading	Focus on teaching points: sentence structure, parts of speech, word usage, etc.	
			After reading	Revisit the text or have student reread. Reinforce teaching points. Engage student in a discussion. Comprehen-sion skills can be reinforced by referring to the text.	

Table 5.12 Advance Lesson Plan: Shared Reading

Lesson Component	Purpose	Materials	Implementation		Observations/ Assessments
Shared reading 10 minutes	Select a purpose for the shared reading based on learning objectives, strategy, or modeling technique to be taught (remember, you read with the student).	Select an informational text to focus on text structure (or other specific strategy and/or teaching points).	Before reading	Introduce text with learning objectives as focus. Have student discuss what is known about the topic and what he or she would like to learn about the topic. Introduce and discuss text structures. Walk through the book and point out different types of text structures. Model how the text structures help you understand the topic before reading the text.	Observe how student attends to text structures during shared reading. Listen to how student participates.
			During reading	Focus on teaching points: text structures. Model how text structures provide guidance and information during reading. Model how text structures can help clarify information in the text.	
			After reading	Revisit the text or have student reread. Reinforce teaching point: text structure. Engage student in a discussion. Comprehension skills can be reinforced by: showing the student how to turn the main headings and subheadings into questions. Have students return to the text to answer the questions.	

Summary

This chapter provides basic information about reading to and with your student during tutoring. Literacy instruction involves the continuous dynamic interplay of the text, the reader, the tutor, and the contextual format or setting. This dynamic force takes into account text genres, the reader's and tutor's cultural and linguistic background and literacy repertoires, and the context (i.e., the safe or risk-taking situation in which the learning and teaching take place). Whether participating in a read aloud or a shared reading event, all of the procedures listed in the lesson plans take time and practice to learn. Remember to begin with the lesson plan that fits your learning needs first. Please review your initial responses and add or revise them based on what you have learned.

Pre-Reading Questions

What are the benefits of conducting a read aloud and a shared reading? What do you think might be difficult about selecting an appropriate book to read? How would you plan an interactive reading lesson for an English learner? What would be some key ideas to implement? Why?

Chapter 6: Teaching Reading
Guided Reading

How did you learn to read? Do you remember? Some of us remember exactly how we learned to read and can tell stories about learning the sounds of letters, reading with family members, or moving around the classroom according to our reading group. Others, however, do not remember learning how to read at all. They "just did it!" Not all readers have the same experiences; some struggle with reading, dislike reading, and avoid it as much as possible. Maybe they did not like the books they were given to read, maybe they had a hard time cracking the letter and sound code, or maybe they were not really taught how to read. As a reading tutor it is important that you understand how good readers read. It is also important that you be able to break down the ways to teach reading. We believe everyone is a reader; they just have not found the right book to read!

Purpose of the Chapter

The purpose of this chapter is to assist you in understanding what guided reading is, why it is important, and how to use guided reading during your tutoring instruction. Guiding reading relies on you, the tutor, knowing how your readers read, what they can read, and what they like to read. To be able to teach them in ways that help them make reading progress, you also have to consider what it means to be a guide or coach. Think about something you are not able to do well. What would you need to improve? What types of things would you like your teacher or coach to show you? For Julie, it is snow skiing. She loves to ski. But she is not a good skier, depending on how you measure a good skier (if a good skier is someone who never falls and can ski all day). She is very happy to ski on the easy green slopes, with their slight downward angles, in the company of cautious fellow skiers. She can relax and enjoy the snow for hours while she confidently scoots down the mountain. Julie has been skiing on the green slopes for

10 years, yet she has friends who are great skiers. They love to ski as fast as they can down the expert black slopes. They are convinced she has a deep desire to join them and often try to talk her into going with them. She *can* ski on the black slopes, but it is not pretty. She has to snowplow (keeping her knees together tightly while pressing into the snow) the entire time so she does not go too fast and fall. She hates to fall. Skiing on the black slopes makes her hate skiing. It makes her tired. It makes her want to go home. It makes her never want to ski again. The black slopes are frustrating for her. Therefore, after 10 years of skiing on slopes that are too easy and slopes that are too hard, she was left at the same skiing level. She had made no progress. For her to make progress to the next level, the blue slopes, she had to take ski lessons. She had bad instructors and great instructors. The ineffective instructors issued orders and waited for her to perform. Yelling unhelpful hints such as "Don't lean when you turn!" and "Look up!" While she did my best to follow the dictated orders, she often fell back into leaning and looking down at her skis, because she didn't know why she shouldn't lean or where to look when she wasn't looking at the snow beneath her skis. The great instructors talked to her, asked her what she knew and what she liked about skiing. They asked her to ski down a run as they watched her before they began to tell her what she was doing wrong. They modeled what she was doing wrong and then modeled what she should be doing. They also skied in front of her as she followed in their tracks, explaining what they were doing and asking her to do the same. They skied ahead of her and then watched her ski, talking to her the entire way and cueing her just before she turned, telling her, "Shift your weight to the outside of your left foot, now even out your weight." Over time, her skiing slowly improved without her hating skiing and feeling she had to risk her life to learn how to ski on the tougher runs. It is important to note she was not learning how to ski on the black slopes; they were too hard for me. She was also not learning to ski on the green slopes; they were too easy for her.

Guiding students' reading is very similar to any type of good instruction or coaching. To be a good teacher of reading you need to know your students. You need to understand their likes and dislikes, their habits, and their fears. You need to make sure they are not too tired or intimidated by the text. You have to model what good readers do and give them support as they read and improve, saying the right thing at the right time to them when they get stuck on a new word or don't understand what they are reading. Ineffective reading teachers can continually issue orders such as "sound it out" every time a reader is stopped by an unfamiliar word. While this may help readers in some cases, it can also hurt their progress by not teaching them multiple strategies to use when sounding out a word does not work. Have you ever tried to sound out the word *they* by putting the individual sounds *t-h-e-y* together? This is difficult to do because the consonant digraph "th" makes a unique sound. Just as Julie needed to be taught to ski on the blue slopes to improve, readers need the right text to challenge their learning and they need an attentive teacher to coach them as they read. Before you read this chapter, please take a moment to answer the pre-reading questions that follow. Record your answers so when you are done reading you can go back and review what you have learned.

Pre-Reading Questions

How do you know about how we read?
How do you know which book to select for your student?
How can you help students when they do not know a word?
What do you do if a reader does not understand what he or she read?

Several key terms will be important as you plan and guide readers in reading. Understanding text levels and how they can adjust to reader ability, the role of meaning, decoding, and grammar in reading, and how strategies and tutor prompting help students read will be covered throughout the chapter. Each term is defined for you and specific definitions will be highlighted within the text.

Key Terms

Text Levels	Meaning/ Semantics	Decoding/Visual	Grammar/Syntax
Prompting			

As you begin to tutor, you will be able to use these terms to describe how your readers are reading and how you can respond as a tutor. Being a good reading tutor requires understanding the relationship between students and the texts you are asking them to read. It also means being a guide for them as they read. The following sections will detail what guided reading is, why it is important, and how you can use it as you tutor. Each essential element of guided reading is covered in detail for beginning, intermediate, and advanced tutors. Video examples will illustrate how guided reading is taught to readers at various levels and with unique needs.

What Is Guided Reading?

Guided reading is designed to assist readers as they read instructional level text (Clay, 1991b; Fountas & Pinnell, 2012). The role of you as the tutor is to select text that is not too easy nor too hard and to support the reader as he or she reads. The goal of using texts slightly above the students' reading level is to assist them so their reading improves and they move up reading levels. Guided reading is reading instruction focused on how you as a tutor are able to coach readers before, during, and after they read. It is a very active and interaction-based type of reading instruction characterized by you setting up the new text your readers will read, setting up a goal for the learners before they read, praising their successful use of reading strategies, and prompting them to use new strategies as they read.

Why Is Guided Reading Important?

Guided reading is the heart of reading instruction. Explicit prompting and support of the reader is key to improving his or her reading ability. Reading with students and modeling reading strategies for them makes the act of reading explicit and clear. Reading can be seen by struggling readers as an invisible and mysterious process. Guiding students as they read and explicitly teaching them how to read is an important way to break down the process of how to read for readers.

How Is Guided Reading Used in Tutoring?

In tutoring instruction, guided reading is used to help readers develop their use of reading strategies so they can become independent readers of a variety of texts. Guided reading is a chief component of tutoring and should be used in every tutoring session. Students selected for individual tutoring sessions are identified as struggling; therefore, one of the goals of the tutoring sessions is to improve their reading. Reading improvement is typically measured by what level text the reader is reading. Guided reading is the most direct method for teaching reading strategies. Each tutoring session should devote at least 10 to 15 minutes to guided reading instruction.

Essential Elements of Guided Reading

Each essential element of guided reading instruction works toward assisting the reader as he or she reads an instructional level text. To be successful with your reader you will need to understand the essential elements of guided reading and how they can help you tutor.

1. Knowing student's reading level (relying on prior assessments)

2. Selecting instructional level text

3. Understanding the three cueing systems

4. Understanding how to prompt

All of these elements are key to teaching reading. While it is helpful to read to students and model aspects of reading for them (see Chapter 5), teaching them to use specific strategies in challenging text is the way to help them improve. Even accomplished readers can benefit from guided reading strategies and they use them unconsciously. Read the following text excerpt aloud.

CASE REPORT[1]

A 60-year-old white man presented with a temperature of 103.8° F (39.9° C), shaking chills, nausea, headache, neck stiffness, and severe back pain. History was significant for recurrent uric acid stones initially treated with extracorporeal shock wave lithotripsy in March 1999, and then with laser lithotripsy in July. After the latter procedure, the patient was discharged home on levofloxacin and began preventative treatment with acetazolamide and allopurinol. He was readmitted to the hospital the day of discharge with a temperature of 104.0° F (40.0° C), presumably due to a partially treated urinary tract infection. The patient had taken the initial 300 mg. allopurinol orally only a few hours earlier. Broad-spectrum antibiotics were given, and the allopurinol and acetazolamide were discontinued. An extensive fever evaluation was negative. The patient recovered from this acute episode and was doing well at a scheduled follow-up in August. At that time he was restarted on allopurinol and acetazolamide. Soon after taking 300 mg. allopurinol orally, the patient returned to the hospital and was diagnosed with a drug reaction (versus possible urosepsis).

During hospitalization, the patient became confused and agitated. Neurology was consulted to evaluate the altered mental status, persistent headache, and neck pain. Infectious disease and internal medicine services were also consulted. White blood count was 9,500/mm^3 (normal 4,300 to 10,800) with 85% neutrophils (normal 45%–74%). Urine and blood cultures were negative. Chest

1   David A. Duchene, Christopher P. Smith, and Richard A. Goldfarb, from "Allopurinol Induced Meningitis," The Journal of Urology, vol. 164, no. 6, p. 2028. Copyright © 2000 by Elsevier B.V. Reprinted with permission.

radiograph and computerized tomography of the head, abdomen, and pelvis were normal. Electroencephalogram showed a slow occipital rhythm and diffuse slowing of background activity, which indicated a diffuse disturbance in brain function. Cerebrospinal fluid analysis revealed protein 149 mg/dl (normal 25–50), glucose 62 mg/dl (normal 40–70), 33 red blood cells/ml (normal 0–5), and 74 white blood cells/ml (normal less than 5) with 53% neutrophils (normal 0%), 29% lymphocytes (normal 60%–70%), 6% monocytes (normal 30%–50%), 1% eosinophils (normal 0%–7%), and 11% basophils (normal 0%–2%). Cerebrospinal fluid venereal disease research laboratory and cryptococcal screen was nonreactive with no acid-fast bacilli present. Cerebrospinal fluid culture and antigens for group B streptococci, group B Haemophilus influenzae, Neisseria meningitidis, Streptococcus pneumoniae, and Escherichia coli were negative. Test results were consistent with an aseptic meningitis syndrome caused by allopurinol drug reaction. The patient was asymptomatic and afebrile after allopurinol was discontinued, and was discharged home in good condition. (Duchene, Smith, & Goldfarb, 2000, p. 2028).

How did you do? Did you read every word? What did you do when you came to a word you did not know? Were you able to understand the paragraph? Most readers will read texts and use reading strategies such as rereading sentences or phrases, sounding out new words, skipping words that are difficult, or in the most extreme cases giving up completely. If you had a teacher guide you through this text, it would be a very different experience. The teacher would have done the following:

- Introduced the text to you (Clay, 1991).
- Taught you a few key words that might be unfamiliar to you.
- Assisted you as you read.
- Reviewed the reading with you once you were done.
- Possibly reread the text to increase your fluency and comprehension.

These are key implementation components to guided reading lessons. For example, an introduction to this text would involve discussing the patient as a case study, describing that he was admitted to the hospital due to a high fever. He was tested for various diseases. Words such as *allopurinol*, *lithotripsy*, and *meningitis* would be defined prior to reading. Where allopurinol is a drug used to reduced uric acid often related to kidney stones, lithotripsy is a procedure used to remove kidney stones, and meningitis is an illness causing swelling around the brain and spinal cord. As you read, the tutor would help you pronounce unknown words or prompt you to make a good guess at a word and then move to the next word. The tutor would ask you about the meaning of the text. If you were made aware the text is about a severe drug reaction to allopurinol, it could help you as a reader determine how to read it. While this text is probably readable in that we can read the words, it is usually what we call a challenging text. Having someone guide your reading before and during reading can assist you with tackling more difficult texts, which is the essence of guided reading instruction.

Please view the following video for an example of a guided reading lesson.

Video 6.1

Reader Reading Level

Reader reading level is key to planning guided reading lessons. Each reader can be evaluated using Informal Reading Inventories and running records (see Chapter 4). Once the student's reading level is determined, instructional level texts are selected to plan and provide instruction. It is important to note that reader reading levels can change quickly and constant observation should be a part of planning guided reading sessions.

Instructional Level Text

The type of text used in reading tutoring is an important factor (Fisher & Frey, 2014). There are two ways to evaluate the difficulty levels of texts: (1) how easy or hard the text is for the reader, and (2) how easy or hard the text is in relation to other texts. In reality, reading can be easy or quite difficult for anyone. You can read a magazine with ease. You can also read books or articles related to reading. Yet, if you had to read a tax return instructions to read, you might struggle. You might avoid reading them. You might clean your entire house instead of reading them. If you did try to read them, it would be because you had to. You might reread sentences several times, start to read segments aloud slowly so you could try to understand them, and you might try to find someone with knowledge about taxes to help you. Anyone can struggle with reading, even the very best readers. The level of text difficulty matters. While guided reading is connected to students reading texts at their instructional level, that same level can be a moving target. For example, many of us can read news stories. The type of story and how well we can read it will always vary. Some people keep up with pop culture news. They can read a story about a celebrity and not only understand the story but also how that particular story relates to the celebrity's past. They may be able to talk about not only the events in the news story but also what they mean for the celebrity's identity. They have a deep understanding of the content of the text they are reading. They are bringing in background information, knowledge of the vocabulary and context of the story, and are motivated to read and understand it. In the same newspaper, there may be a political story. While the text source is the same, the reader may be able to read the story and recall events read but may not be able to place the events in the larger political context. The reader may also come across new vocabulary words that may not be completely understood. If the reader is not interested and motivated to understand the story, then he or she may skim over it and move on.

Text levels vary. They are unique to the reader reading the texts. As the reader gains more reading skills and knowledge of the content and vocabulary, the same text can move from a frustration to an independent level text. Another aspect of text levels is their measurability by specific criteria. Book publishers, researchers, and exam publishers have devised ways to measure the difficulty levels of text. This view of text levels is static. A text may be labeled as a first-grade level text. Such a text will have only a few sentences on each page, with illustrations or pictures that match what the text is saying. The text will use common, simple words such as *the* or *look.* These leveled systems are helpful in selecting texts because they are somewhat predictable. The complicated aspect of these specific levels is that not all first graders can read first grade level texts. As a reading tutor, most of your readers will not be reading texts that match their grade level perfectly so you will need to understand how to evaluate texts and choose those that best fit your readers.

Each reader is unique. Guided reading depends on finding texts that are at the student's instructional level (Fountas & Pinnell, 2012). Similar to Julie's skiing levels where green slopes are easy and black slopes are too difficult, instructional level refers to a level where the learner is slightly challenged. If you want to help your readers improve, you have to expose them to harder texts. The key to making progress is to support them as they read more challenging texts so they learn new strategies and do not become frustrated. Assessing your student's reading (see Chapter 4) will provide a guide for selecting an instructional level text for guided reading. The terms *instructional* level, *frustration* level, and *independent* level are indicators of how well readers are matched to the text they

> *Text Level in Relation to the Reader*
>
> The level of difficulty of a text is shaped by the content as it relates to the reader's knowledge, the vocabulary as it relates to the reader's word knowledge, the complexity of the sentence structure, and the reader's motivation to read it.
>
> *Text Level in Relation to Specific Criteria*
>
> Text level is measured by the type of vocabulary, the frequency of specific words, the complexity of the sentence structure, and the content or genre.

are reading. Frustration level texts leave readers frustrated because they are too difficult. Independent level texts are easily read by the reader, who do not need any help with reading or understanding the text. You want to guide students as they read instructional level texts.

Please view the video example of a guided reading lesson.

Video 6.2

Understanding text levels is an essential element of reading instruction. Carefully chosen texts can provide you with opportunities to assist your readers as they read more challenging texts. At the beginning of your tutoring sessions, you will want to record the text level of your reader using an informal reading inventory and running records (see Chapter 4). Tracking your students' reading levels is key to monitoring their growth. We recommend using a tracking log similar to the one in the appendix.

Instructional Level

Guided reading requires using instructional level texts during lessons to help readers improve. These are texts that are read with at least 90% of the words correct and with good understanding.

Cueing Systems and Strategies

Good readers rely on three cuing systems (Goodman, 1967) as they read: (1) meaning/semantics, (2) decoding/visual, and (3) grammar/syntax (see Chapter 1). Guided reading is designed to address how struggling readers use or do not use these cues as they read (Fountas & Pinnell, 2012). As the tutor, you need to understand what they are and how your reader uses specific strategies related to the cues as they read. Once you understand them, you start to observe your reader's use of them.

Cueing Systems

Meaning/semantics refers to how readers use the meaning of the text as they read.

Many struggling readers are unable to integrate the strategies and do not know how or when to use them. Some readers may just rely on sounding out every word, so they need to learn how to use the meaning of what they are reading and the grammar of the sentence to access the unknown word. This flexibility and integration is automatic with good readers but has to be taught to those readers who are not using the cueing systems well.

Meaning/Semantics

The first cue, meaning or semantics, is related to how readers use their understanding of the content of the text as they read. The following example illustrates how readers might read with an overreliance on meaning or semantics. The sentence in the text is:

I rode a horse.

But the reader instead reads the text as:

I rode a donkey.

As a tutor, you would notice the student is using meaning possibly based on the knowledge that people can ride horses and/or a picture that represents a donkey could be mistaken for a horse. In this case, it is clear the reader is not using visual cues (e.g., the letters *h-o-r-s-e*). On the other hand, they are using grammar; both horse and donkey are nouns and each fits grammatically in the sentence. Although the reader has used meaning if we consider horse and donkey to be close in meaning, the reader has somewhat changed the meaning. Yet overall, the sentence still makes sense and probably makes sense to the reader. Readers who rely primarily on meaning will make many of these types of what we call meaningful substitutions. They read with meaning in mind, and when they are not sure of a word they insert a word that makes sense according to what they understand the reading to mean.

Decoding/Visual/Graphophonic

The ability to sound out words and use knowledge of word parts to read unfamiliar words is important to reading. Readers can use decoding to work through words one letter at a time and can use knowledge of word parts to read new words. For example, the sentence in the text is:

I rode a horse.

But the reader instead reads the text as:

I rode a h-o-r-s-e.

The reader is focused on making the sound of each individual letter. By making each sound the reader is trying to figure out the word *horse*. This strategy also requires that the reader understand the phonics rules that apply. In this case, the reader has simply decoded each letter resulting in the word being read as *horsee*. Not knowing the *o* is r-controlled and makes a new sound and the *e* is silent results in an error. The reader also has to blend each sound together after saying each individual sound. Decoding, or using visual cues, is very effective for readers when the words they are trying to read are phonetically regular. Phonetically regular words are words in which each letter sound is constant and clear, such as in the word *c-a-t.*

Grammar/Syntax

Readers who are able to use their knowledge of syntax or grammar as they read make sure that what they are reading is grammatically correct, nouns are nouns, verbs are verbs, etc. For example, the sentence in the text is:

I rode a horse.

But the reader instead reads the text as:

I sat on a horse.

While the meaning of the text is somewhat different and the word *rode* is replaced by *sat on*, the reader does maintain the grammatical structure of the statement. When readers overly rely on grammar as they read, they often substitute words that fit into the sentence but change the meaning of the sentence and do not visually match the letters in the word.

For the purposes of demonstrating what each reading strategy might look like, we have discussed them separately. Yet readers' strategy use often involves more than one cueing system. Learning to analyze their reading takes time and practice, and you will see that your readers will use a few strategies more frequently than others. When you recognize this, you can begin to prompt them to use all three strategies together as they read.

Please view the video for an example of a guided reading lesson.

> **Grammar/ syntax**
>
> Refers to how readers use their knowledge of language structures as they read.

Video 6.3

Prompting

Once you understand the three cueing systems, you can focus on assisting your readers as they read using specific prompts (Clay, 1991b). Prompting students as they read is one unique aspect of guided reading. It is used as a tool to guide students and direct them to use specific strategies. Prompting is used to promote independence in readers by teaching and reinforcing reading strategy use.

As a tutor, you will use prompts throughout the reading of an instructional level text. They can be used during the book introduction to highlight unique phrases or new words in the text. They are most commonly used during reading to help students when they encounter difficulties. Prompts are the opposite of simply telling the reader the information. While there may be times when you tell a reader what the new word is, in guided reading the goal is to prompt the learner to try various reading strategies so he or she can figure out the word or phrase that is troubling and learn to use the strategy in the future.

Prompting for Meaning/Semantics

Prompts for meaning are used when readers are not using meaning as they read. They include statements such as:

Does that make sense?

What is happening in the story?

These questions are designed to bring readers' attention to the meaning of the sentence and to the story overall. They may be using decoding and grammatical cues as they read. By asking these questions you are teaching them that reading should make sense and that their decoding should also make sense.

Prompting for Decoding/Visual

Prompts for decoding are used to bring the reader's attention to the letters and word parts in the word he or she is reading. They include statements such as:

What does that word start with?

Do you see a part of the word you know?

Readers who are not using visual cues may be substituting words that make sense but are not connected to the actual word. Readers can avoid using visual strategies and try to bring in substitutes that make sense, such as substituting the word *ran* for *walk*. The words do not look similar nor are they spelled the same. When students make this type of error, you can assume they are using meaning instead of visual cues. As a tutor, you want to draw their attention to how to decode or chunk words they are not familiar with to reinforce their awareness of visual strategies.

Prompting for Grammar/Syntax

Prompts for grammar are often tied to meaning, and many students will maintain grammatical correctness as they read unless the text structure is unique and varies from the reader's oral language speech patterns. They include statements such as:

Did that sound right?

Asking readers if their reading sounds correct reinforces the notion that reading should sound correct. It typically mimics speech readers hear.

Overall, understanding how to prompt students as they read is crucial to helping them progress in their reading. Many of these prompts are designed to have students crosscheck their attempts to see whether their approximations are correct. There are several ways to prompt students, and the resource section of this chapter offers additional sources.

Please view the video to see an example of guided reading.

Video 6.4

Guided Reading and ELs

Guided reading involves supportive and structured reading procedures. Engaging English Learners (ELs) in the guided reading process provides strategic and specific reading instruction geared to their individual literacy needs. Selecting leveled text at the EL student's instructional level provides an opportunity to offer scaffolded and guided instruction in areas of need. The various steps involved in guided reading provide the structure to systematically walk the EL student through the text and tailor instruction. Guided reading provides ELs with literacy support in the following ways:

1. activates prior knowledge or helps build an understanding of the text or concepts in the text;

2. provides increased oral language skills;

3. provides structured support in learning and increasing knowledge in the cueing systems: semantic, syntactic, and visual or decoding;

4. provides increased knowledge in word recognition; and

5. supports comprehension skills.

As you plan your lesson for work with an EL student, make sure to provide a well-paced lesson so you do not rush through any teaching or instructional practice. Pacing is important so that EL students have time to process language interactions. Establish set routines so the EL student knows what is expected for each segment of the lesson. Practice speaking and reading clearly throughout the instruction—not just during read alouds. Provide visuals, realia, or use gestures to provide instructional support. And finally, always set and have high expectations for your student.

Please see the following two videos for examples of guided reading with ELs.

Videos 6.5 and 6.6

Teaching and Planning for Guided Reading: Tutor Levels of Knowledge

The following section focuses on five areas of teacher knowledge related to guiding students' reading. Each area is divided into three levels: beginner, intermediate, and advanced. As you progress with your understanding of reading instruction you can refer to the different levels to increase your learning.

Guiding Reading Content Knowledge

Guiding reading content knowledge is focused on understanding the components of the essential elements of reading processes. Table 6.1 provides an overview of the areas covered in this section.

Table 6.1 Guiding Reading Content Knowledge

Essential Elements	Description
Reader reading level	Determined by measuring: • accuracy, • comprehension, and • fluency. Reader reading levels can change over time. Frequent assessment using running records is key to making sure you know the reading levels. Reading level also varies according to book genre and background knowledge. Depending on what type of book is used, reading level can vary dramatically. Multiple assessments should be used to determine the reading level including running records and IRIs.
Text	All texts are written in specific ways and can be analyzed and used to teach different reading strategies. Text types can be used to reinforce decoding, meaning, or grammar. Select a text based on your reader's strategy use. Texts used in lessons should be carefully selected and a variety of genres (e.g., narrative, informational) should be used.
Cueing systems	The three cueing systems readers use when they read: • *Semantics:* Meaning/understanding • *Visual:* Decoding words and pictures • *Syntax:* Using grammatical structure Each reader will rely on some strategies more than others. Identifying a student's strategies is done by using miscue analysis, which examines reading errors and determines what strategies students use the most and then focuses on how to encourage use of other strategies. Retrospective miscue analysis (REA) can be used with students after reading. REA shares running records and miscue analysis with students after they read, explaining their miscues and how they can improve their reading.
Prompts	Teachers use prompts to teach reading strategies to students as they read. Prompts should be based on miscue analysis and used during guided reading to teach readers to use additional cueing systems.

Guided reading pedagogical content knowledge is focused on the ways guided reading is taught.

Table 6.2 Guided Reading Pedagogical Content Knowledge

Essential Elements	Description
Reader reading level	Reader's reading level determines how you will approach your instruction.
Text	Select a text your reader cannot read on his or her own. The text needs to be at the student's instructional level or one they can read with support.
Cueing systems	Teaching the cueing systems is a part of guiding students' reading. Prompts are used as students read to help them learn the cueing systems.
Prompts	The basic prompts are: • *Semantics:* Does that make sense? • *Visual:* What sound does that make? Or Does that look right? • *Syntax:* Does that sound right?

Guided reading curricular knowledge is focused on the curricular materials associated with guided reading and their use.

Table 6.3 Guided Reading Curricular Knowledge

Essential Elements	Description
Reader reading level	Reader reading levels are labeled in many ways: • Grade level • IRI level by company (e.g., DRA) • By program (e.g., Reading Recovery) • Lexile There are many sources that coordinate the levels for you.
Text	Types of instructional texts: • Basal readers • Leveled readers • Decodable texts • Informational texts • Literature
Cueing systems	Instructional texts are designed to encourage the use of specific cueing systems. You can select a text that provides your students with the opportunity to use certain strategies.
Prompts	Many programs will list prompts for you (e.g., Fountas & Pinnell).

Planning for Guided Reading

Planning for guided reading is complex and involves understanding how students read and how to prompt them as they read. This section is devoted to providing you with sample lesson plan configurations at the beginning, intermediate, and advanced levels based on your understanding of guided reading. Each lesson sample and its accompanying template is designed to provide a framework for organizing your instruction.

If you are just starting to tutor, you need to focus on making sure you are covering the basics of guided reading. The lesson plan format that follows lays out a basic guided reading lesson. Italicized text indicates how you should implement the activity.

Table 6.4 Beginner Lesson Plan: Guided Reading

Lesson Component	Purpose	Materials	Implementation		Observations/ Assessments
Guided reading 10 minutes	Reader reads, uses visual, contextual, and syntactic strategies and responds to text.	Text	Book introduction	*State the book's main idea.* *Let the reader skim through the pages and share his or her thoughts.*	Was the book at the student's level? How was the student's fluency? What strategies did you notice the reader use? Did the student understand the text?
			New word focus	*Select one word that the reader may not know.* *Read the word to the student and explain its meaning.*	
			Reading	*Support the reader by using prompts when he or she stops at an unknown word.*	
			Comprehension check	*Ask the reader to retell the events or facts in the text.*	
			Rereading	*Have the reader reread the text or an excerpt of the text.*	

As you become more comfortable with using guided reading, you will need to refine your teaching. The lesson plan that follows adds more options for your lesson.

Table 6.5 Intermediate Lesson Plan: Guided Reading

Lesson Component	Purpose	Materials	Implementation		Observations/ Assessments
Guided reading 10–15 minutes	Reader reads, uses visual, contextual, and syntactic strategies and responds to text.	Text	Book introduction	*Ask the reader to predict what the text is about based on the title and cover.* *State the book's main idea in one sentence.* *Let the reader skim through the pages and share his or her thoughts.* *Clear up any misconceptions the reader may have.* *Ask the reader to confirm or reject his or her prediction.*	Was the book at the student's level? What was the student's accuracy rate? How was the student's fluency? Was it consistent throughout the book or varied? What strategies did you notice the reader use? What did your miscue analysis reveal? Did the reader understand the text? Was the reader's retelling accurate and thorough? Did he or she answer specific questions correctly?
			New word focus	*Select one word that the reader may not know.* *Read the word to the student and explain its meaning.* *Have the reader find the word in the text and read the word in the sentence.*	
			Reading	*Support the reader by using prompts when he or she stops at an unknown word. Reinforce and praise when the reader uses appropriate prompts.*	

	Strategy review		*Review and praise one reading strategy the reader used.*	
	Comprehension check		*Ask the reader to retell the events or facts in the text. Ask the reader follow-up questions about details and interpretations of the text.*	
	Rereading		*Review target strategy use and have the reader reread with a focus on the strategy.*	

Once you become advanced in your tutoring, you will want to deepen your instruction. The following lesson plan template provides more challenging teaching ideas for you to use.

Table 6.6 Advanced Lesson Plan: Guided Reading

Lesson Component	Purpose	Materials	Implementation		Observations/ Assessments
Guided reading 10–15 minutes	Reader reads, uses visual, contextual, and syntactic strategies and responds to text.	Text	Book introduction	*Ask the reader to predict what the text is about based on the title and cover. State the book's main idea in one sentence. Let the reader skim through the pages and share his or her thoughts. Clear up any misconceptions the reader may have. Ask the reader to confirm or reject his or her prediction. Review the strategies the reader should focus on as he or she reads the text.*	Was the book at the student's level? What was the student's accuracy rate? How was the student's fluency? Was it consistent throughout the book or varied? What strategies did you notice the reader use? What did your miscue analysis reveal? Did the student understand the text? Was the student's retelling accurate and thorough? Did he or she answer specific questions correctly?

Lesson Component	Purpose	Materials		Implementation	Observations/ Assessments
			New word focus	*Select one word that the reader may not know.* *Read the word to the student and explain its meaning.* *Have the reader find the word in the text and read the word in the sentence.* *Have the reader construct the word using magnetic letters or write it on a whiteboard.*	
			Reading	*Support the reader by using prompts when he or she stops at an unknown word.* *Reinforce and praise when the reader uses appropriate prompts.* *Anticipate and prompt before or as a student comes across an unknown word to reinforce use of a prompt.*	
			Strategy instruction	*Review and praise one reading strategy the reader used.* *Teach a new strategy based on the reading.*	
			Comprehen-sion check	*Ask the reader to retell the events or facts in the text.* *Ask the reader follow-up questions about details and interpretations of the text.*	
			Rereading	*Explicitly teach and model a key strategy by showing the reader his or her miscue.* *Have the reader reread the text emphasizing the target strategy.*	

These lesson plan samples are intended to assist you as you develop your teaching skills. They move from the simplest type of lesson to much more complex plans.

Summary

Guided reading is a key component of reading instruction. It provides the reader with opportunities to read challenging texts with intense tutor support. The specific guided reading elements of understanding your student's reading level, how to use text levels, and how to identify reading strategies and prompt the student as he or she reads are key to your success as a reading tutor. Remember to see yourself as a coach, constantly observing and responding to your readers as they read. It is okay to interrupt them at times to praise and reinforce their strategy use or to prompt them to use a strategy they are working on learning. As they make progress, keep in mind the importance of assessing their reading using running records to ensure you are using instructional level texts. Keep in mind the goal of tutoring is to assist your reader and help him or her move to reading more difficult texts. Now that you have read the chapter and viewed the videos, revisit your answers to the reading prompts at the beginning of the chapter. Check your understanding of these questions and how you can use the information to plan and teach your student.

Pre-Reading Questions

What strategies do you use when you read a difficult text?

How do you know which book to select for your student?

What type of assistance can you provide when the student does not know a word?

In what ways can you assist an EL if the student does not understand what she or he read?

Chapter 7: Teaching Reading
Reading Independently

Remember the last book you stayed up late reading? Was it one of those books that you kept telling yourself, "Just one more page and then I will go to sleep"? But you couldn't put it down until you finished it. Or have you ever read a book that upon finishing you wanted more to read and could not believe you were at the end of the story? How could the author end the story like that? There must be one more page or perhaps a sequel? Reading informational text can have the same effect. The factual information might captivate the imagination so much that after reading the book you find yourself seeking more texts about the subject so you can delve deeper and gain more knowledge about the topic. Good books and genres we enjoy reading do that to us: They make us want to keep reading. In our busy lives we probably feel that reading for pleasure is a luxury, and with all the things we must do there is just is not enough time to sit and read quietly for even 10 minutes. The truth is the more we read the better readers we become. Want to get more muscle tone? Go to the gym more often and workout using weights. Want to focus on a specific area to tone? There are different machines, weights, and exercises you can use to get in shape. Reading is the same way. Reading different genres will help students understand different text structures and be prepared to tackle a variety of texts. Reading widely and often will help your student become a better reader. Make sure to model independent reading so your students "catch you" reading during a portion of independent reading time. Independent reading does not mean you sit back and read the entire time; you will also engage your students prior to reading to discuss strategies they can use while reading and questions they may have after reading.

Purpose of the Chapter

This chapter discusses independent reading and its effect on improving a child's reading ability. Teaching students how to select books they are motivated to read and are able to read on their own is also discussed. Independent reading is not as easy as having the student take a book off the shelf and read it. There are several factors involved in selecting the appropriate text for independent reading just as there are for read alouds and shared reading. Setting a purpose for independent reading is important as well. The student needs to know why he or she will be sitting next to you as you both read quietly for the set amount of time you have allotted. Are you having the student read for pure enjoyment then briefly discuss the text? Or will there be some type of response or recall required during and after the reading time? Students need to know that all elements of the lessons you design have a purpose to assist them in becoming a more proficient reader. Before you read this chapter, please take a moment to answer the pre-reading questions that follow. Record your answers so when you are done reading you can go back and review what you have learned.

Pre-Reading Questions

Why should students read on their own?
How does a student select a book to read independently?
What does it mean to assist students as they read independently?

A few of the key words that will be discussed in this chapter are listed below.

Key Terms

Independent Reading Level	Lexile Measures	Genres

What Is Independent Reading?

Independent reading is a specific time you have allotted in the lesson when the student reads a text on his or her own. The text selected for this reading time should be a text the student can read with little to no support. Independent reading during guided reading should be a book that you know is at the student's independent reading level or one he or she is reading at about 98% word accuracy. You can also think of it this way: For every 100 words of text there should be no more than two miscues. It is important to include independent reading during the tutoring session to allow the student time to read and reflect, and to practice strategies you may have taught in the lesson or in a previous lesson.

Independent Reading Level

The student's independent reading level is a text the student can easily read on his or her own without much support.

Why Is Reading Independently Important?

Why is independent reading important? Allowing for independent reading during the lesson provides you with the opportunity to model strategic reading and thinking that students can use as they read on their own and it gives students the opportunity to read silently and to rehearse the metacognitive strategies you have taught during other parts of the lesson. Independent reading also provides practice in reading fluently, improves sight word recognition, and internalization of comprehension strategies and cueing systems. While reading silently, students are not worried about making sure they decode each word properly; they are not concerned with oral precision and can focus on complete comprehension of the text. In essence, reading independently allows the student to put into practice all of the techniques, strategies, and behaviors you have worked on and modeled throughout tutoring.

Please view the video for an example of a student reading independently.

Video 7.1

How Do You Select a Text for Independent Reading?

How do you feel about the last book you were told you had to read (most likely) for one of your classes? If you found the topic interesting and the information engaging you may have enjoyed the book. The reality is that most students in elementary schools are assigned specific readings and materials to read and are rarely given choice over selecting a book to read during instructional time. Students may have some choice of selection for books they check out at the school library and take home to read, or to keep in their desk to read if they finish their class work early. Researchers have found that having the choice to pick a book on their own helps motivate students to read (Turner, 1995; Moss & Hendershot, 2002). Helping a student select an appropriate text should begin by looking at their assessment information such as the Qualitative Spelling Inventory or QSI (Bear, Invernizzi, Templeton, & Johnston, 2008) or Informal Reading Inventory or IRI (see Chapter 4 for more information). The IRI will provide information on your student's word recognition skills and comprehension abilities, usually in a grade-level format. The QSI will provide you with a spelling level that also correlates with a reading level. But most important, it will give you a glimpse into how the student hears sounds and uses patterns or other skills to spell the words. This information should be used as a starting point. You should also know your student's interest after administering the reading interest inventory, conducting several read alouds, and from your conversations with your student about texts. All of this information should be used to guide your student in selecting an appropriate text. Look at your student's IRI level and match it to the leveled book chart. You can have your student select a book from the leveled books you have read previously, a newly leveled book that would fall within his or her independent reading level, from a previous read aloud or shared reading book, or a new selection from the classroom library. If your student has decided to read a book that is not from the leveled section of the library, make sure to check the book's Lexile measure (using Lexile.com or a free Lexile app) to check for reading level appropriateness. The Lexile system measures text complexity using a readability formula to provide an appropriate level for the book.

Most readability formulas look at word difficulty, word length (number of syllables), and sentence length and structure to assess the complexity of the text. Some of the assessments students take at school provide Lexile measures for their reading ability. You might

The Lexile System

The Lexile system can be used to find a book leveled at your student's approximate reading level.

want to ask your students if they know their Lexile level range. While the assessments we use do not produce a Lexile measure, you can still enter the book title into the Lexile.com website and get a text measure for the book. As an example, if you type in Lois Lowry's *Number the Stars* the Lexile.com program generates a Lexile level of 670. Using the Lexile to grade correspondence chart you will see that a 670-level book would be within the fifth-grade range. Lexile levels provide a range for each grade level but are not exact. Another method the student can use is to open a book and read a few paragraphs to see how many unknown words he or she encounters. Too many unknown words may mean the book will prove a difficult text. Encourage your students to select a book they can read on their own or is at a "just right" level for them. Your student can use Tompkins's (2013) "Goldilocks" strategy to select a book. If your students have difficulty making a decision, try modeling the process for them using a think aloud. Here is a possible script for the think aloud:

Too Easy Book Selection

> *I think I want to read* Diary of a Minecraft Zombie *(Herobrine Books, 2015; Lexile 590) but using the Goldilocks strategy (Tompkins, 2013) I know I am an expert on the topic. I looked at the first few pages and I know all the words on the pages I scanned, and there aren't as many words on a page as I think a chapter book should have. I think this book is too easy for me so I am going to try another book.*

Too Hard Book

> *I picked the book* If I Ever Get out of Here *(Gansworth, 2013; Lexile 870). I know someone who read it and liked it but after looking at the first few pages I think the text is too small. There are a lot of words on each page and there were quite a few words I didn't know. I think I will put this book back because it might be a little too hard for me to read on my own.*

Just Right Book Selection

> *I think I might try* P.S. Be Eleven *(Williams-Garcia, 2013; Lexile 770). I haven't read this book before but I have read other books by this author. The book cover caught my attention and I would like to learn more about the three girls on the cover jumping rope. After flipping through the first few pages I feel confident I can read most of the words. There are a few words I am sure I have read before and can figure out using the strategies I have learned like read on and using context clues. This book seems like a "just right" level for me so I will read this book during independent reading.*

Once a student has selected a text or you have preselected a text for the learner, explain the purpose of independent reading and what independent reading time will look like during the lesson.

Why Should a Student Read a Variety of Genres?

The word *genre* is a French word that means a type or category of literature. In children's literature, several distinct literary genres divide fiction into further categories such as picture books, fantasy, traditional literature, science fiction, realistic, and historical fiction. Nonfiction or informational text is another genre with several categories or distinct types. Examples include autobiography, biography, history, science, letters, documents, and journals. Poetry is another genre that consists of different styles or forms of poetry such as sonnets, limericks, lyrical poems, ballads, acrostic, and haiku to cite a few. Genres such as traditional literature, fiction, nonfiction, and poetry have specific text structures that are used to create the text and help identify the type and style. Knowing how text structures work in different genres can serve as a road map through a text and help the student recognize the type of text he or she is reading and often how to tackle or read the text. If students are reading a nonfiction or informational text, they can assume the information in the story is accurate and true. They will look at headings, subheadings, pictures, graphs, maps, captions, and other text structures to help them understand the text and content and determine the story's accuracy.

Exposing your students to a variety of genres during tutoring and explaining how the text is structured will help them enjoy the text more; of more importance, it will help them to better comprehend the story, information, or poem. Students should read from—and become familiar with—a wide variety of texts and text structures to become more proficient readers and, ultimately, writers. As a tutor, you should make a conscious effort to purposefully select a variety of genres to read with—and to—your student. As your students mature as readers, assist them in selecting a variety of text types for their independent reading.

Please view the video to see an example of a student reading an independent level book.

Video 7.2

How Do You Assist Students as They Read Independently?

Monitoring Student Text Selection

As cited previously, text choice and introducing different genres to the student is important toward improving his or her reading repertoire. Monitoring your student's text choice is the best way to assure students are reading books at their independent level and from diverse genres. One way to monitor their book selection is through a reading log such as the following table. After each independent reading session fill out the log in each appropriate section.

Table 7.1 provides an example of an independent reading log.

Table 7.1

INDEPENDENT READING LOG						Anecdotal Notes/Comments
Book Title	Date	Pages Read	Book Level	Selection Self/Teacher	Genre	

By keeping track of students' selections you can monitor the types of text they are reading independently and suggest different genres if you notice them only sticking to one or two specific types. Students, just as adults, tend to gravitate toward certain book types or styles they enjoy and are uncomfortable trying new genres. Besides assisting them with text selections, teaching them different independent reading behaviors will also be beneficial.

Promoting Student Growth

As a tutor, you should model your reading behaviors when you read independently with the student; this will help him or her develop independent reading skills. During independent reading, you can take a few minutes to model a reading strategy, such as rereading for clarification, and then guide the student step-by-step through the process. Once the student has practiced the strategy, have the student show he or she understands the strategy by demonstrating it to you. Then proceed with both you and your student reading independently for the allotted time allowed.

English Learners (ELs) and Independent Reading

As addressed previously in this chapter, it is important for all students to read text from and be exposed to a variety of genres but especially so for English learners. ELs need to understand that depending on the genre, a book may be formatted and written differently. For example, historical fiction may include sections in which the English language is written to represent a different time period or era and may not sound or look like the English language they hear every day. The academic language in informational text may also be challenging for ELs. Informational text may have vocabulary words that ELs recognize and understand when used in fiction or narrative, but the words may have a completely different meaning when used in nonfiction. It is important to make sure ELs are exposed to different text structures and book genres so they will know how to tackle the text when they come across it during independent reading. Independent reading can also help ELs build their vocabulary and academic language skills, so it is essential to schedule independent reading time during each tutoring session. Remember that independent reading is an active and interactive process and must be as well planned as any other section of tutoring.

Please view the video to see an example of an EL student reading an independent level book.

Video 7.3

Teaching and Planning for Independent Reading Behaviors: Tutor Levels

The following section looks at independent reading as it pertains to content, pedagogical and curricular teacher knowledge (see Chapter 1 for more details). Each area is divided into beginner, intermediate, and advanced. As you develop your understanding of the essential elements in independent reading you can refer to the different sections to increase your understanding.

Independent Reading Content Knowledge

Modeling independent reading content knowledge is based on understanding the essential elements involved in the process of reading independently.

1. Knowing your student's independent reading level.

2. Being able to select different genres and texts in children's literature.

3. Understanding how to model independent reading behaviors.

4. Knowing how to assist your student in setting goals for independent reading.

Table 7.2 provides an overview of the areas covered in this section.

Table 7.2

Essential Elements	Description
Independent reading levels	Determined by: • Informal Reading Inventory • Running records • QSI A student's independent reading level is a text he or she can read on one's own with little to no support or at 98% or above word accuracy and 95% or above comprehension. Using information from oral reading, silent reading, spelling assessments, and observational anecdotal notes you should be able to determine your student's independent reading level. Reading skills will vary depending on text genre, structure, and content so continuous assessment and observations are necessary to accurately determine your student's independent reading level.

Essential Elements	Description
Genre and text selection	Most students have a favorite type of text or genre they feel comfortable and successful reading. Knowing the different genres in children's literature to select appropriate text for your student is important in expanding their reading knowledge of text structures, vocabulary, and comprehension. Fiction, non-fiction, and poetry are broad terms used to describe children's literature. Each of these terms is divided into several specific genres. These types of texts have specific characteristics and text structures that must be pointed out to your student.
Different independent reading behaviors	There are different ways to model independent reading behaviors and a variety of ways to implement the actual process. Knowing why you have included independent reading in your lesson plan should be spelled out in your rationale.
Setting goals for independent reading	All instructional strategies have a specific purpose. Of most importance, teaching your students to set specific goals for their independent reading will make the process strategic, meaningful, and motivational.

Independent Reading Pedagogical Content Knowledge

Independent reading pedagogical content knowledge is focused on the ways independent reading is taught.

Table 7.3 Independent Reading Pedagogical Content Knowledge

Table 7.3 Independent Reading Pedagogical Content Knowledge

Essential Elements	Description
Independent reading levels	The student's independent reading level will assist you in planning instruction.
Genre and text selection	Guide the selection of a specific genre and text for independent reading.
Different independent reading behaviors	Understand the independent reading behaviors your student exhibits and the behaviors you need to model.
Setting goals for independent reading	Assist students in setting goals for independent reading. Model before, during, and after reading strategies and behaviors.

Independent Reading Curricular Content Knowledge

Independent reading curricular knowledge is focused on the curricular materials associated with independent reading.

Table 7.4 Independent Reading Curricular Content Knowledge

Essential Elements	Description
Independent reading levels	Independent reading levels are individualized and will not be indicated in curricular materials.
Genre and text selection	Some reading programs have leveled text that can be used for independent reading. It is best to use books or texts that provide students choice and most likely will not be part of a prescribed program.
Different independent reading behaviors	Specific independent reading behaviors may or may not be mentioned in curricular materials.
Setting goals for independent reading	Curricular materials may have established goals for the reading materials available in the curriculum but it is best to establish individual goals for your student.

Planning for Independent Reading

Planning for independent reading involves understanding your student's reading level, reading interest, reading behaviors, and different genres in children's literature. This section provides you with sample lesson plans at the beginning, intermediate, and advanced levels based on your understanding of independent reading behaviors. Each lesson sample and its accompanying template is designed to provide a framework for organizing your instruction.

Table 7.5 Beginner Lesson Plan: Independent Reading

Lesson Component	Purpose	Materials	Implementation		Observations/ Assessments
Independent reading 10 minutes	To promote independent reading behaviors and strategies in students.	Independent level reading material/ book	Before reading	Make sure the book is at the student's independent level and will be interesting to the student. Assist student in setting a purpose for reading.	Observe how student attends to the text during independent reading time. Basic Retell: Who: character(s) Where: setting What happened

Lesson Component	Purpose	Materials	Implementation		Observations/ Assessments
			During reading	Remind students to use the reading strategy cue cards if they encounter a word they don't know.	
			After reading	Have student provide a basic retell: who, where, what.	

Table 7.6 Intermediate Lesson Plan Independent Reading

Lesson Component	Purpose	Materials	Implementation		Observations/ Assessments
Independent reading 10 minutes	To promote independent reading behaviors and strategies in students.	Self-selected independent level reading material/book	Before reading	Assist students in the process of self-selecting a text at their independent reading level. Remember to review the selection strategies (too easy, too hard, just right). Assist student in setting a purpose for reading.	Observe how student attends to the text during independent reading time. Have student provide a more detailed retelling: Who: characters Where: setting What happened: Beginning Middle End
			During reading	Remind students to apply word-attack strategies if they come across a word they do not know.	
			After reading	Have student provide a more detailed retelling: Who: characters Where: setting What happened: Beginning Middle End	

Table 7.7 Advanced Lesson Plan Independent Reading

Lesson Component	Purpose	Materials	Implementation		Observations/Assessments
Inde-pendent reading 10 minutes	To promote indepen-dent reading behaviors and strategies in students.	Self-select-ed indepen-dent level reading material/book	Before reading	Assist students in the process of self-selecting a nonfiction text at their independent reading level. Review text structures for cause and effect, or problem solution nonfiction text.	Observe how student attends to the text structures in nonfiction texts during indepen-dent reading time. Have student provide written details from the story in his or her response journal.
			During reading	Remind the student to apply the compre-hend-sion strategies taught in previous lessons to help the learner understand difficult text.	
			After reading	Have student provide a short, written review on the material read in the response journal. Have student share his or her work.	

Summary

These simple lesson plan samples are intended to assist you as you develop your teaching practice. The lessons are developed to provide lesson ideas from beginner to advanced levels. Independent reading helps a student practice reading and to use strategies previ-ously taught, and in providing the student with choice in selecting texts. Please review your initial answers and revise to include new information.

> **Pre-Reading Questions**
>
> Why should students know about text structures in nonfiction texts?
> How can you assist students as they evaluate and self-select text?

PART IV: WRITING TUTORING COMPONENTS AND LESSON PLANS

The fourth section focuses on writing instruction and how to plan and implement each part of the tutoring program. Each chapter covers a specific type of instruction, explains its purpose, and ties it to teaching English learners, followed by sample lesson plans for beginning, intermediate, and advanced tutors. Chapter 8 discusses the language experience approach and interactive writing, Chapter 9 describes how to write with students, and Chapter 10 covers independent writing.

Chapter 8: Teaching Writing
The Language Experience Approach and Interactive Writing

How did you learn to write? Do you remember? Writing can be viewed as a mysterious talent, something that some people have and others do not. Some people write constantly; they may keep a journal, write for their job, or use social media and blogs to share their thoughts while others do not see writing as a part of their life at all. Understanding how writing works can be difficult for students and for teachers. At times people tend to measure writing by spelling and grammar and only see the details of the mechanics of writing, while others focus on the message in the writing and look for meaning in what they write. Just as young students may gravitate to reading or try to avoid it, writing with elementary students is similar. It all depends on how students view writing. Do they think writing is spelling perfectly with beautiful handwriting? Or, do they see writing as a way to share their ideas and experiences with others? As a tutor, you will need to understand how these views of writing can help and hurt students' progress and what you can do to make writing meaningful and enjoyable to all young writers. We think all students are writers because each one of us has something to say.

Purpose of the Chapter

This chapter is designed to show you what modeled writing is, why it is important, and how to use modeled writing during your tutoring instruction. Modeled writing is part of writing instruction that assists writers by modeling various types of writing, and allowing students to observe and understand the actual act of putting words onto paper. Modeled writing is led by you, the tutor, based on what you know about your student's strengths, weaknesses, and comfort level with writing. It is important for you to know their oral language skills, how they spell, what they like to talk about in relation to their own knowledge and experiences. Since modeled writing consists of you modeling writing for your student, it is important that you are a good writer and that you can explain how you write. Try to remember the first time you were learning something. Typically, before we all try to learn something, we have some type of exposure to it—we have seen someone else do it, we have an idea of what it is, and what the end product looks like. For example, if you are learning how to cook. You can look at a cake, cut a slice, taste it and know it is made of eggs and flour, and yet have no idea how to make one. You can read a recipe and by reading and following directions make a cake on your own, but the best way to learn to bake a cake, due to a lack of experience and confidence as a baker, is to watch someone bake a cake and explain what he or she is doing and why. This is what in education we call a think aloud. By modeling and thinking aloud, or explaining activities while doing them, experts can help new learners understand techniques and reasons for each step. In baking cakes, it is very important to use eggs and butter at room temperature to make sure the batter has more air in it and the cake is lighter. It is also important to not overmix the batter, etc. While all of these ideas can be read in a recipe, watching someone make a cake while commenting and demonstrating the consistency of the batter is more informative. Modeling and using a think aloud model as you write for students provides the same type of specific support for students learning to write. You must understand your student's needs and be sure you explain how and why you are writing certain words as you create stories, poems, letters, or reports. More traditional modes of teaching writing provide prompts or ideas and then require students to write with little modeling. In our tutoring sessions, you will model various types of writing and explain the process to your students. Before you read this chapter, please take a moment to answer the pre-reading questions that follow. Record your answers so when you are done reading you can go back and review what you have learned.

Pre-Reading Questions

What do you know about how writers write?
How can you help students when they do not know how to write?

Key Terms

| Modeling | Think Aloud | Language Experience Approach | Interactive Writing |

The terms above will be key to your understanding as you plan to model and explain writing. Understanding how to model different types of writing and how to use thinking aloud as an instructional strategy will be the cornerstones of this chapter. Two specific methods of modeling writing will be detailed as well: the language experience approach (Schwartz, 1975) and interactive writing (McCarrier, Pinnell, & Fountas 1999). Each term is defined for you and specific definitions will be highlighted within the text. As you begin to tutor, you will be able to use these terms to describe how you can respond as a tutor. All students can benefit from modeled writing and the following sections will detail what modeled writing is, why it is important, and how you can use it as you tutor. Each essential element of modeled writing is covered in detail for beginning, intermediate, and advanced tutors.

What Is Modeled Writing?

The purpose of modeling writing is to allow writers to see how writing is produced, from creating ideas to a final polished product. In general, this means that you as the tutor are writing for the student and describing what you are thinking and doing and why. You are making the process of writing letters and words on a page visible by talking to your student before, during, and after you write. Your responsibility is to understand the content areas related to writing (see Chapter 3) and bring those to life for your student. There are various terms and ways to model writing, and for our purposes we are relying on two predominant instructional methods: the language experience approach and interactive/shared writing.

Why Is Modeling Writing Important?

Modeled writing is crucial due to its explicit examples of how to write. By modeling and explaining each step of the writing process to students, you are giving students support by demystifying what writing is. Writing for students allows them to see how writing depends on thinking about your topic before writing, how writers draft and make changes as they write, how they focus on meaning and then attend to spelling and punctuation in later drafts. It also can show students how writers change their minds, rely on pieces of writing they have already seen to understand new forms such as poetry, or how writers bring their knowledge or use research as they write. Without modeled writing, students can be left to observing others write with little idea of how the writer produced a final product and all the work that goes into writing. It also demonstrates how writing can be improved.

How Is Modeling Writing Used in Tutoring?

In tutoring instruction, modeled writing is used to assist students in their understanding of how writing strategies work so they can become independent writers of many types of texts, from poetry and narrative to reports and arguments. Modeled writing does not have to be used in every tutoring session. The main reason for using modeled writing is to show students how to do writing tasks they are unable to complete on their own. It is most often used with emergent writers and spellers, ELs and when teaching students a new genre of writing (see Chapter 3). You should carefully evaluate your student's writing as it relates to your writing lesson objectives and goals.

Essential Elements of Modeling Writing

Each essential element of modeled writing instruction works toward assisting the writer as she or he observes how to write specific texts. To be successful with your student you will need to understand the essential elements of modeled writing and how they can help you tutor.

1. Know the student's writing abilities (relying on prior assessments).

2. Understand the developmental levels of writing.

3. Be able to write the various types of writing.

4. Understand how to think aloud and prompt while modeling writing.

All of these elements are key to teaching writing. We know it is important to engage students in writing activities; showing them how to use specific strategies can improve their writing substantially. Most tutors will keep asking students to write and list all types of possible topics when in reality what the student needs is to learn how to write. The first step to writing is to watch someone write and listen to them explain how they are forming their ideas. Modeling writing tasks include the following:

*   Introduce the type of writing to the student.

*   Talk about the student's ideas before writing anything down.

*   Explain how the student knew how to spell words as he or she wrote.

*   Reread their writing several times throughout the task.

*   Talk about their ideas as they continue.

These are key implementation components to modeled writing lessons. For example, an introduction to the writing task would include talking about the type of writing and sharing ideas orally about what might be written and why. Writing components such as what to write and in what order would be explained by you. Then when starting to write, you would talk about what students were thinking and how they might sound out words that are difficult to spell. The tutor would stop now and then to reread the writing and cross out words not needed or that could be replaced by better words. Words or ideas may be added along the way with explanations as to why. You may add sentences, change ideas, or revise spelling as you write and discuss your process to the student. Modeling writing helps students understand the ways writers construct text explicitly and clearly.

Writer Developmental Level

Developmental levels of writers are important to understand as a teacher of young writers. As detailed in Chapter 1, young writers are not only in the process of learning how to read letters they are also learning how to put letter sounds together to express their ideas. Abilities of young writers can range from students who are able to write *dog* correctly to those who spell *dog* with just the letter *d*. Some young writers feel comfortable writing all of their ideas down quickly and fluently while others stop and start and then backtrack, struggling to get thoughts down at all. Before any type of writing instruction, it is crucial to determine where your student's developmental level is at and what he or she should be taught.

Table 8.1 Developmental Writing Stages

Stage	Description
Random marks	The beginning of writing is often a series of random marks that children make when given a writing instrument. These random marks are often made on walls, furniture, toys, and other nontraditional writing surfaces.
Drawing	Children have learned they can convey meaning with writing. They will describe their drawing.
Scribbles	Scribbles are an important stage in writing. They demonstrate that children know that writing moves left to right and returns. Children can often "read" their scribbles and use pictures to remember what the scribbles say.
Copying	Copying environmental print is a stage where children are remembering the print they are exposed to. They may copy words they know and words they do not know. It's important to move children beyond this stage.
Random letters	As children become exposed to letters, they will incorporate them into their writing. At this stage, the letters may not be associated with the corresponding sounds and children will usually not be able to read their writing once they are done.
Early invented spelling	Following the use of random letters, children will begin to use letter-sound associations as they write. They may use the first letter/sound of each word and then begin to use more letters as they begin to encode the sounds they hear as they write. Many children at this stage can be seen mouthing or sounding out the words as they write. An important step in writing development, this demonstrates their mastery of the concept of the alphabetic principle of letter-sound relationships.
Full invented spelling, transitional spelling	At this stage, most of the writing can be read phonetically despite the number of spelling irregularities. Children are now making educated guesses in their writing and have mastered some of the rules for the language. This stage demonstrates their understanding of phonics well.
Conventional spelling	Spelling is clearly read and follows conventions.

Adapted from Teale 1987, as cited in Lapp, Flood, Brock, & Fisher (2006), pp. 287–289.

Writing can be evaluated using writing samples and spelling inventories (see Chapter 4). Please note that writing is assessed in two major ways: (1) how students use the process of writing (including drafting and spelling), and (2) how students are able to write the different genres of writing. Once the student's writing level is determined, writing tasks are selected to plan and provide instruction. It is important to note that student writing levels can change quickly and constant observation should be a part of planning activities.

Developmental Level in Relation to the Writer

Young writers' developmental levels are based on their ability to draft their ideas fluently, their knowledge of spelling, their use of their oral language vocabulary, the complexity of their sentence structure, and their ability to express ideas in sequence.

All students vary in their writing level, and their writing will appear different based on the task and type of writing they are asked to do. Ensuring you are closely observing their work is key to making good instructional decisions as you plan your writing lessons.

Types of Writing

There are many types of writing. We are relying on personal narratives, report or research writing, and opinion or argument writing. In modeling writing, the most important thing to know is what each type of writing is and how you can model each one. Even kindergarteners can learn the difference between writing a story and writing all the facts they have learned about reptiles. As the tutor, it is your job to know how these writing types are produced and how each is adjusted to your student's developmental level goals. Some students will have an easier time writing a report about a specific topic than writing a piece of fiction.

Writing Level in Relation to Specific Genre

There are many types of writing. We are relying on personal narratives, report/research writing, and opinion/ argument writing.

Each type of text serves a different purpose and has its own unique organization, vocabulary, and style. The point of modeling each type is to introduce students to the genre by stating the purpose of the type, showing them how to plan for writing, showing them what it looks like, and showing them how to draft, revise, and edit. Breaking down each type of writing task for students relies on modeling and thinking aloud for them. As indicated earlier, modeling is simply the act of doing an activity for the purpose of showing it to others. In modeling writing, you are writing the type of text you want the students to produce. While you are modeling writing, you are also thinking aloud for your student and explaining what you are thinking and doing. This thinking aloud allows students to hear how you, as an author, are thinking about all of the aspects of writing, ideas, words, spelling, etc.

Understanding how to model and think aloud for students is an essential element of writing instruction. Carefully selected writing activities will provide you with ways to assist your students as they learn to compose all types of texts. There are two primary activities we will use to model writing for students in our tutoring sessions: the language experience approach and interactive writing.

Think Aloud

Thinking aloud involves talking about all aspects of writing, including ideas, word choice, sentence structure, and spelling. It allows students to hear how authors think as they write.

Language Experience Approach

The language experience approach (LEA) to writing focuses on having the student dictate a story or report to you as the tutor. Before writing you should select a specific type of writing and be familiar with all aspects of the purpose, style, and format of the genre. As a part of prewriting in the process model (see Chapter 3), you will want to engage the student in a conversation about the topic. You may want to show the student an example of the type of writing as well. If you are introducing a new genre to a student, you need to make sure you have read an example of the type of writing to the learner and discussed the various aspects of the writing before asking the student to come up with his or her own. You might also decide to write your own piece for the student. This is also especially helpful to you as a tutor; it ensures you understand the writing task and can compose one yourself before trying to teach it to students. If your purpose is to allow the student to come up with any idea, then the focus is on assisting him or her with coming up with an idea—and working on helping the student on writing and spelling, explaining through thinking aloud as you write.

> *LEA*
>
> LEA allows students to dictate their writing ideas as you write for them. It provides a model of writing and helps students understand the process of writing and spelling as they observe you writing.

Many young writers struggle with one or more of the following issues when asked to write. Some have difficulty deciding on what to write and some struggle with spelling and punctuation. The following two sections present ways to assist students with understanding what content to write and how to use their knowledge of letters and sounds to produce words on the page.

Please view the video to see an example of a language experience approach lesson.

Video 8.1

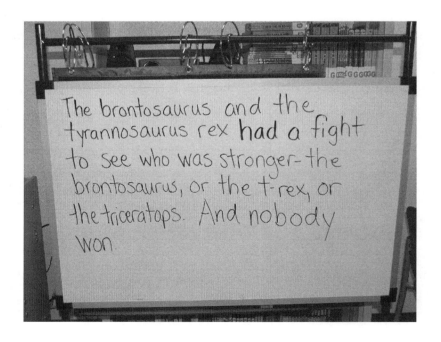

Writing Content

The first step in using LEA is to determine the topic of the writing activity. Once you have assessed your student's strength and weaknesses, you will plan your lessons. If you want to help the student work on how to transfer his or her ideas to paper and learn how to spell, you will let the student decide on the topic. For example, you might ask the student to write about a favorite activity. If the student voices a fondness for swimming, you would ask the learner to say that in a complete sentence. If the student struggles, you might provide an example and state, *I like to read*, as you write your sentence. Once the learner comes up with a first sentence orally, you restate it to the student.

When working with emergent writers it is important to model good handwriting, follow their oral language exactly, and model correct spacing, spelling, and punctuation. You want students to see how their ideas are formed and stay true to how they speak. The purpose of LEA is not to teach correct grammar that can be noted and taught at a later time, but to demonstrate how the act of writing is related to the act of speaking.

If you are working on a specific type of writing with a student who is beyond the emergent level, you can modify your approach to include how to write specific types of texts. For example, if you are working with a student who is comfortable writing about personal experiences, but rarely wants to write about other topics, you can work on writing explanatory or report texts. This may involve reading books about frogs, discussing frogs, and using the Internet to research frogs. Once the student has a clear understanding of frogs you might ask the learner to think about what he or she knows about the subject. You may model taking notes, using a graphic organizer such as a Venn diagram, or making a list of facts. Part of LEA, as used here to teach certain writing genres, is to model not only how to write, but how to prepare to write. As the student dictates his or her knowledge about frogs, you will write exactly what the learner says. Once the student's ideas are recorded, you can begin to ask how the student wants to order the facts, what information the learner wants to include, and how he or she wants to structure the work—as a report, a newspaper article, or as a PowerPoint presentation.

As you use LEA, keep in mind the requirements that you write for the students, that you maintain their message, and that they read their work. You must also remember to think aloud as you write. You want to talk about each decision you are making, how you're able to spell words, why you are using certain words over others, and what you are thinking about as you work. The focus on content is important but for many the mechanics of writing are just as difficult. The next section explains the importance of how to teach spelling and punctuation when working with emergent and struggling writers.

Please view the video to see another example of LEA.

Video 8.2

Writing Mechanics

Just as students use their knowledge of letters and their sounds to read new words, writers use that same knowledge to write. Writing is a process (see Chapter 3). As such, while students are writing their first drafts, you will want to encourage them to use invented spellings of words so they do not get bogged down in spelling and forget their ideas. One way to model this, and to show students how words are produced by using letter sounds, is to model how you sound out words when you spell. LEA works well for modeling spelling because, as a tutor, you can explain how words are made up of certain sounds, and you can show spelling patterns that may not be heard. For example, if a student states, *I like to swim*, you can model the *I* sound and then follow up by sounding out *like* (l-i-k) and telling the student there is a silent *e* as you write the letter *e*. By explaining your spelling, you are showing students how the words we speak are made up of sounds we can write down and at times there are some letters that are silent. These early examples of how to spell are done within the actual writing time and are short and specific only to the writing worked on at the time. More formal spelling instruction will occur in other tutoring lessons. LEA writing is simply a way to model and address skills naturally and quickly. During this time, you will also talk about any punctuation marks you use and why you are using them. In the video observe how the tutor thinks aloud about spelling and punctuation as he or she models writing for the student.

LEA is entirely focused on writing for students. You as their tutor are writing down each word they say, commenting on why you are spelling words with certain letters, and why you are adding punctuation. Students never hold a pencil as you write; they are watching and learning as you bring their words to the page.

Interactive/Shared Writing

Interactive/ Shared Writing

Interactive/shared writing is sharing the writing task with students to assist them with unknown words or difficult aspects of texts.

Interactive or shared writing is different from LEA in that you and your student each have a pencil or marker and are writing together. The goal is to allow students to write what they know and be there for them to fill in the word blanks or parts of words they do not know. Just as with LEA, before you can both write together you need to ensure the message is clear. Discuss the writing task with the student in detail as a part of pre-writing (see Chapter 3) and then state one sentence at a time as you write to make sure you know what the student wants to write.

Once the student has stated what she or he wants, you both say the sentence and then begin on the first word. Interactive writing is a word-by-word, letter-by-letter activity, with each word and each letter written and discussed. As you write, you must be careful to let students use their knowledge and only step in when they are unsure what to write. For instance, you may know the student knows how to spell the word *I*, so you let him or her write *I* on the page. The student may know that *swim* begins with *s* so you allow the learner to write *s*. You also know the *w* in *swim* will be difficult for the student so you

step in and say the next sound in *swim* is *w* as you write the letter *w* for the student. This continues until the text is complete.

The key to effective interactive writing is to know what your student knows so you can be prepared to write when he or she needs you. You also should use thinking aloud as a tool to explain what you are doing. Interactive writing can assist students quickly, and once they are shown a spelling or punctuation skill they will often remember it and use it on their own. As a tutor, you will use prompts throughout the writing of a text to move students' writing abilities forward. Two key prompts to reinforce during interactive writing are prompting for spelling and punctuation. At times genre and meaning will come up as you and the student read and reread the writing together. You need to make sure you are helping your students check their ideas and that their writing makes sense. If you are teaching a specific genre, then you will also need to make sure the genre is clearly a part of the writing activity.

Please see the video example of an interactive writing lesson.

Video 8.3

Prompting for Content

Prompts for content are used when writers are not following the style of the genre they are using or not keeping on topic as they write. They include statements such as:

Does that idea fit in the story/report?

What is happening here in your story/report?

These questions are designed to bring the writer's attention to the meaning of the sentence and to the story overall. Writers need to continually read their work as they write to check for meaning. And by asking these questions, you are also teaching your students that their writing should make sense.

Prompting for Spelling and Punctuation

Prompts for spelling and punctuation are used to bring the writer's attention to the letters and parts of the word they are reading. They include statements such as:

What does that word start with?

What goes at the end of a sentence?

Writers who need assistance with spelling and punctuation are then able to respond to these prompts. If students are not able to answer the prompts then you should note that and prepare a mini-lesson on areas that are not mastered.

Using LEA and Interactive Writing with Ells

LEA and interactive writing are both appropriate strategies to engage ELs in authentic writing activities. LEAs encourage ELs to make personal connections and to use oral language skills to express their thoughts and ideas in a supportive environment. Tapping into the EL student's understanding of an experience or text and then modeling the writing process using the student's words is a powerful process. LEAs provide ELs with literacy support in multiple ways:

1. increased oral language skills as they engage in a discussion about the topic;

2. active and modeled spelling instruction as the EL's words are written down;

3. listening skills as they listen to their story or sentence read aloud; and,

4. syntactical skills as they watch you assemble their words in proper order.

While LEAs use the student's words, thoughts, and ideas, the student does not actually write. In interactive writing the student actively participates in the writing process. The writing process is scaffolded as students are encouraged to contribute their spelling and word knowledge by writing the letters or words they know. This process is supportive as the tutor "shares the pen" and helps the EL complete words or sentences. Interactive writing provides ELs with literacy support in the following ways:

1. increased oral language skills as they engage in a discussion about the words, spelling, and syntax;

2. participation in activating word knowledge, spelling, and syntax to write words and complete sentences; and,

3. comprehension and syntactical skills as they compose and write sentences and paragraphs that make sense.

Continual and increased use of modeled writing processes will help ELs increase their understanding of word knowledge, writing structures, and oral language proficiency. As you plan your lesson to work with an EL student, make sure to provide a well-paced lesson so you do not rush through any teaching or instructional practice. Pacing is important so that EL students have time to process language interactions. Establish set routines so the EL student knows what is expected for each segment of the lesson. Practice speaking and reading clearly and not just during read alouds but throughout instruction. Provide visuals, realia, or use gestures to provide instructional support. And finally, always set and have high expectations for your student.

Please view the video for an example of LEA with an EL.

Video 8.4

Teaching and Planning for Modeled Writing: Tutor Levels of Knowledge

The following section focuses on areas of teacher knowledge related to modeling writing for students. Each area is divided into three levels, beginner, intermediate, and advanced. As you progress with your understanding of writing instruction you can refer to the different levels to increase your learning.

Modeled Writing Content Knowledge

Modeling writing content knowledge is focused on understanding the components of the essential elements of the writing processes:

1. Knowing the student's writing abilities (relying on prior assessments).

2. Understanding the developmental levels of writing.

3. Being able to write the various types of writing.

4. Understanding how to think aloud and prompt while modeling writing.

Table 8.2 provides an overview of the areas covered in this section.

Table 8.2

Essential Elements	Description
Writing level	Determined by measuring: • oral language, • spelling, and • fluency. Writer abilities change over time. Frequent assessment using oral language assessments, spelling inventories, and observation is key to making sure you know the writing ability of your student. Writing skills vary according to type of writing and knowledge of phonics and spelling patterns. Multiple assessments should be used to determine students' writing needs.
Developmental levels of writing and spelling	All writers are continuing to develop their skills. In elementary instruction, developmental writing levels focus on oral language patterns, spelling, and fluency. Understanding where students' developmental levels are is key to planning lessons so they can continue to make progress in these areas. Writing activities should include a variety of genres (e.g., narrative, informational) with extensive modeling.

Types of writing for elementary students	There are three types of writing used in elementary instruction: • *Narrative:* personal narratives, fiction • *Explanatory/Informational:* nonfiction, reports, newspaper articles • *Argument/Opinion:* thesis, persuasive writing Each type of writing has a unique style and purpose. It is important to know how each type is organized, what type of information is required, and what vocabulary is used and why. Understanding the aspects of each type is required before teaching students how to write each genre.
Thinking aloud and prompting	Using prompts to teach writing strategies to students as they write is necessary to provide a clear model for them. Prompts should be based on knowing student skills and knowing the type of writing task.

Modeled Writing Pedagogical Content Knowledge

Modeled writing pedagogical content knowledge is focused on the ways modeled writing is taught.

Table 8.3 Modeled Writing Pedagogical Content Knowledge

Essential Elements	Description
Writing level	Writer developmental levels determine how you will approach your instruction.
Developmental levels of writing and spelling	Select a writing task your writer cannot complete by himself or herself. Be familiar with the developmental level expected skills.
Types of writing for elementary students	Understand the types of writing and what makes them difficult for your student. Be prepared to step in when necessary to model and explain.
Thinking aloud and prompting	The basic prompts are: *Content:* Does that makes sense? *Spelling:* What sound does that make? *Spelling for Older Students:* Does that look right?

Modeled writing curricular knowledge is focused on the curricular materials associated with modeled writing and their use.

Modeled Writing Curricular Knowledge

Table 8.4 Modeled Writing Curricular Knowledge

Essential Elements	Description
Writing level	Writing levels are not specifically indicated in most lesson materials. Standards and student skills may be listed but there are no prepared activities due to the nature of writing and the need to let students produce ideas. There are examples of writing products to view and adapt to your student.
Developmental levels of writing and spelling	Language experience approach and interactive writing are typically used for emergent and early writers. They can be adapted for fluent and transitional writers, especially if you are introducing a new type of writing and your student needs modeling and support.
Types of writing for elementary students	Instructional manuals and prompt sheets exist and can help you break down the steps in process writing as it relates to the different types of writing. Using too many preset activities can result in making students do worksheets. It is best to allow students to come up with writing ideas as you help them; it keeps them interested.
Thinking aloud and prompting	Many programs will list prompts for you (e.g., Tompkins).

Planning for Modeled Writing

Planning for modeled writing is complex and involves understanding how students write and how to model writing for them. This section is devoted to providing you with sample lesson plan configurations at the beginning, intermediate, and advanced levels based on your understanding of modeled writing. Each lesson sample and its accompanying template is designed to provide a framework for organizing your instruction.

Beginner Lesson Plan: Modeled Writing

If you are just beginning to tutor, you will want to focus on making sure you are covering the basics of modeled writing. The lesson plan format that follows lays out a basic modeled writing lesson and can be adapted and used with LEA or interactive writing. Italicized text indicates how you should implement the activity.

Table 8.5 Beginner Lesson Plan: Modeled Writing

Lesson Component	Purpose	Materials	Implementation		Observations/ Assessments
Modeled writing 10 minutes	To model writing for students.	Paper and marker or computer	Prewriting discussion	*State the purpose of the writing task. Let the student talk about the topic.*	What does the student know about the type of writing? How is the student's oral expression of ideas? How is the student responding to the print as you write? Was the student able to read his or her writing?
			Decision about text to be written	*Discuss the ideas in detail and assist the student with deciding exactly what to write.*	
			Writing	*Write as the student dictates to you. Think aloud and explain how you are spelling and forming sentences.*	
			Rereading	*Have the reader reread the text he or she wrote.*	

Intermediate Lesson Plan: Modeled Writing

As you become more comfortable with using modeled writing, you want to refine your teaching. The lesson plan below adds more options for your lesson.

Table 8.6 Intermediate Lesson Plan: Modeled Writing

Lesson Component	Purpose	Materials	Implementation		Observations/ Assessments
Modeled writing 10–15 minutes	To model writing for students	Paper and marker or computer	Prewriting discussion	*State the purpose of the writing task. Show a model of the type of writing you want the student to write. Let the student talk about the topic.*	Does the student know enough about the topic to be able to write? Does the student need support with ideas before writing? Is the student able to remember his or her sentences during dictation or forget or change them? Is the student following along as you write? Is the student able to read his or her words? Can the student evaluate his or her writing ideas?
			Decision about text to be written	*Discuss the ideas in detail with the student. Assist the student with deciding exactly what to write.*	
			Writing	*Write as the student dictates to you. Think aloud and explain how you are spelling and forming sentences.*	
			Strategy review	*Review and praise one writing skill the writer is learning.*	
			Genre check	*Ask writers to read their writing. Ask readers if their writing makes sense.*	
			Rereading	*Have readers reread the text they wrote.*	

Advanced Lesson Plan: Modeled Writing

Once you become advanced in your tutoring, you will want to deepen your instruction. The following lesson plan template provides more challenging teaching ideas for you to use.

Table 8.7 Advanced Lesson Plan: Modeled Writing

Lesson Component	Purpose	Materials	Implementation		Observations/ Assessments
Modeled writing 10–15 minutes	To model writing for students	Paper and marker or computer	Prewriting discussion	*State the purpose of the writing task.* *Show a model of the type of writing you want the student to write.* *Let the student talk about the topic.* *Guide the student's ideas by modeling using a prewriting strategy (listing, graphic organizer).*	Does the student know enough about the topic to be able to write? Does the student need support with ideas before writing? Is the student able to remember his or her sentences during dictation or forgets or changes them? Is the student following along as you write? Is the student able to read his or her words? Can the student evaluate his or her writing ideas? Can the student evaluate his or her writing in relation to the type of writing? What skills did the student learn? What should be taught next time?
			Decision about text to be written	*Discuss the ideas in detail with the student.* *Assist the student with deciding exactly what to write.* *Write a draft for the student to model drafting.*	
			Writing	*Write as the student dictates to you and discuss how writers move from prewriting to drafting.* *Think aloud and explain how you are spelling and forming sentences.* *Emphasize key aspects of writing in your think aloud that you want the student to learn to do independently.*	
			Strategy review	*Review and praise one writing skill the writer is learning.* *Demonstrate the skill by going back to the writing sample and explaining how it was used during the writing.*	
			Genre check	*Ask the writer to read his or her writing and compare it with the sample.* *Ask the reader whether his or her writing makes sense.*	
			Rereading	*Have the reader reread the text he or she wrote.*	

These lesson plan samples are intended to assist you as you develop your teaching skills. They move from the simplest type of lesson to much more complex plans.

Summary

Supporting students' writing through modeling and careful scaffolding is crucial to their development. Ensuring that you as a tutor understand writing levels and how to write yourself is key. Writing instruction has to be informed, preplanned, and flexible so you can respond to what students bring to writing tasks. Please review your initial responses and revise them based on your new learning.

Pre-Reading Questions

How are students' developmental levels related to teaching modeled writing?
How can you use LEA and interactive writing to teach different types of writing?
What should you do if a student refuses to write?

Chapter 9: Teaching Writing

Writing with Students

As we discussed in Chapter 8, writing can be a mysterious process. Guiding students as they write is a powerful way to assist them in improving their writing and supporting them during the actual act of writing. Writing with students means you will go from the very beginning of the writing process, prewriting, to the final aspect, publishing with the student. You will become a writing partner and coach for your student and help him or her write all types of writing. As you guide the student's writing you will focus on the process of writing. Process writing is based on how real writers write (Graves, 2005). When you had writing assignments for school or work, how did you approach them? Did you procrastinate and wait until the last minute? Did you write one draft and then turn it in? Or did you write an outline, talk about your ideas with others, and then rewrite your piece several times before turning it in? All of us have some type of experience with writing. Knowing how you approach writing is important, along with knowing how writers write. When you tutor, you will want to think about all stages of the writing process and how you can break writing into manageable steps for students. As we stated earlier, all students are writers because they all have ideas to share. Your job as a tutor is to help them work through the writing process so they can share their message with others.

Purpose of the Chapter

The purpose of this chapter is to demonstrate both the stages of the writing process and the various types of writing students are asked to complete in schools. Guided writing is part of writing instruction that shares the process of writing from beginning to end by asking questions and providing immediate feedback to students. Guided writing puts the pen in the student's hand while you guide his or her writing by providing examples, posing questions, and providing feedback on the learner's progress. Guiding student writing requires that you not only understand your students' writing abilities but also what they know about the type of writing they are asked to do. You guide their writing knowing what they might need help with and what might be difficult for them based on your observations and assessments. Think about your writing methods. If you were asked to write a fictional story how would you approach it? Would you be able to immediately sit down and write a 6,000-word narrative story? Would the story include well-developed characters, a descriptive setting, and a conflict and resolution? If you had to write an opinion piece for the newspaper on a current event could you write a reasoned, clear argument with supporting evidence? These may be simple tasks for us as grownups but most writers spend time planning and preparing to write. They read and think about their ideas, find supporting information, and then draft ideas by taking notes or making an outline. A final written product from fiction to opinion to textbook goes through many versions before it is published. This process of publishing requires several steps and is common for writers. The more writers use a process to write, the better their writing and the more they understand the topic. Guiding student writing involves helping students through each stage of the writing process as they work on a variety of types of writing. Students need support as they write and require clear guidance throughout the process. In our tutoring sessions, you will guide students through the writing process as they write narratives, informational texts, and opinion pieces. Before you read this chapter, please take a moment to answer the pre-reading questions that follow. Record your answers so when you are done reading you can go back and review what you have learned.

Pre-Reading Questions

What do you know about the stages of writing?
How can you help students write different types of writing?

The key terms that follow will be crucial to your understanding as you plan to guide your student's writing.

Key Terms

Narrative	Informational	Opinion	
Prewriting	Drafting	Revising	Editing

This chapter will hone in on how to guide each specific step of the writing process and the features of each of the three types of writing (Calkins, 2014) you will teach. All of the terms are defined for you and the definitions highlighted within the text. All levels of students can be helped using guided writing. The next sections describe what guided writing is, why it is important, and how you can use it as you tutor. Each essential element of guided writing is defined for beginning, intermediate, and advanced tutors. Videos will show you how guided writing is used to assist students with all types of writing no matter what their writing level.

Please view the video of a student going through the writing process.

Video 9.1

What Is Guided Writing?

The main goal of guided writing is to provide clear and immediate feedback and assistance to students as they are writing. As a tutor, you are sitting next to the student and making sure the learner knows what type of writing he or she is doing and what steps are needed to complete the piece. Your role is very similar to a coach, one in which you are prompting in the moment and helping students based on the task you have decided to teach that particular day. To do this, you must understand the three types of writing (narrative, informational, and opinion) so you can steer students in the right direction, and you must understand the stages of the writing process. These two areas will be covered in the following sections.

Why Is Guiding Writing Important?

Guided writing supports students during their writing to help them improve. Some writing models simply ask students to come up with ideas and write. Guided writing is the opposite; it asks you as a tutor to be there to guide students as they write. You will help your students as they come up with writing ideas, you will show them examples of the type of writing they are working on, and you will help students draft by asking them questions. Guided writing is the actual teaching of writing as students write. For instance, if a student writing an informational text about dogs begins to add events that belong in a fiction text, then you are there to ask why the information is being added and can assist the student in revising the work so it relates to the genre she or he is writing. Guided writing avoids giving students feedback on work they have already done, which can result in discouragement. Instead, it gives students feedback in the moment, allowing them to learn as they write.

How Is Guided Writing Used in Tutoring?

During tutoring instruction, you will use guided writing to help students as they write. You will have preselected the type of writing you intend to teach and will have a clear goal related to what stage of writing your student is working on. You will use guided writing in each tutoring session. You might decide to prewrite and draft one piece over a day and then use the next few days to revise and edit. Or you may want to work on one piece of writing over the course of a week. Some students may need to just draft something and not worry about spelling, so you therefore might work on drafting for a few weeks and then select one to work on for publication. Your tutoring decisions depend on how well your student is writing and on what she or he needs to learn.

Essential Elements of Writing with Students

Each essential element of guided writing instruction works toward assisting writers as they write specific texts. To be successful with your student you will need to understand the essential elements of guided writing and how they can help you tutor:

1. Knowing student's writing abilities (relying on prior assessments).

2. Understanding the developmental levels of writing.

3. Being able to write the various types of writing.

4. Understanding the writing process stages.

These elements are important to teaching writing. Students need clear goals and instruction as they write; guiding them as they write can advance their writing skills significantly.

How did the student write? Why? What did the tutor do and say as the student was writing? Guided writing depends on constant interaction and discussion. There are several steps in the writing process and attending to each step is key. Typically, a guided writing session will include the following:

- Introducing the type of writing to the student (showing/reading a model text).
- Discussion about student ideas before writing anything down.
- Drafting ideas in the form of a graphic organizer, list, or outline.
- Rereading the student's writing several times throughout the task to revise his or her work.
- Editing the student's writing for spelling, conventions, and grammar.
- Publishing the student's work for others to read by making a presentation (Power-Point, typed book, video presentation).

All of these components should be a part of your writing instruction. You may work at the student's pace; it is not possible to complete all of these stages in one lesson. You have to plan for the writing tasks based on the number of times you meet with your student, how he or she is doing with the writing task, and what is needed to improve. You may find that your student can write narratives well and it takes very little time for the learner to come up with an idea and draft. On the other hand, your student may struggle with coming up with ideas for informative texts. The student may need to read a text that is explanatory and then discuss how the text was written, or may need help in making an outline and then drafting an informational text. As you learn about your student's writing abilities, you will need to plan according to what he or she needs. Keep in mind that the goal is to teach all stages of the writing process and all three types of writing. Therefore, you want to keep your student moving forward and not just rely on one type of writing.

Writer Developmental Level

Developmental levels of writers are important to understand as a teacher of young writers. Young writers are not only in the process of learning how to read letters they are also learning how to put letter sounds together to express their ideas. Abilities of young writers can range from students who are able to write *dog* correctly to those who spell *dog* with the just the letter *d*. Some young writers feel comfortable writing all of their ideas down quickly and fluently while others stop and start and backtrack, struggling to get any thoughts down at all. Before any type of writing instruction, it is crucial to determine where your student's developmental level is and what he or she should be taught.

Writing can be evaluated using writing samples and spelling inventories (see Chapter 4). Please note that writing is assessed in two major ways: (1) how students use the process of writing (including drafting and spelling), and (2) how students are able to write the different genres of writing. Once the student's writing level is determined, writing tasks are selected to plan and provide instruction. It is important to note that student writing levels can change quickly and constant observation should be a part of planning activities.

Developmental Level in Relation to the Writer

Young writers' developmental levels are based on their ability to draft their ideas fluently, their knowledge of spelling, their use of their oral language vocabulary, the complexity of their sentence structure, and their ability to express ideas in sequence.

All students vary in their writing level and their writing will look different based on the task and type of writing they are asked to do. Ensuring you are closely observing their work is key to making good instructional decisions as you plan your writing lessons.

Types of Writing

There are many types of writing. We are relying on personal narratives, report or research writing, and opinion or argument writing. The skills of writing such as spelling, punctuation, and grammar are consistent across any type of writing. It is important to also know how each type of writing is shaped by its purpose, vocabulary, and style. All students of any age can learn to write narratives, informational texts, and opinions. Young students can write in all of these ways with clear and focused support.

Narratives

Most young students are familiar with narratives; many families and teachers read narratives to students and many films students are exposed to clearly follow a narrative structure. Narratives can include narratives about personal experiences or fictional stories. Narrative structures typically include a sequence of events, a conflict and resolution, and clear characters and settings.

Although narratives might appear to be a simple type of writing, students need support to make sure that they include a well-sequenced and organized story. Exposing students to narrative books and pointing out how the story is organized is helpful. Asking students to find parts of the story and then ways to form their own story with the same parts builds up their writing knowledge. Guiding students step-by-step through the story parts and how they are organized requires discussion and prompting. As a tutor, you may ask students to elaborate on ideas, add more details, or reread to make sure their story makes sense.

Informational

Informational texts are designed to be informative. They have a specific structure. Just as with narrative, students need guidance as they learn how informational texts are set up and organized, and how they define and explain ideas and terms. Often students will need help gaining enough information about a topic to have something to write about. Providing them with prewriting information is key; writing is extremely difficult when students do not know about the topic. During tutoring, you will need to provide students with models of informational texts but also with prewriting activities that provide them with a deep knowledge of the focus area they are writing about.

As you teach students to write informational texts you need to keep their age and writing level in mind and adapt your lessons to their interests and understanding. Students must learn to rely on sources such as other texts, charts, videos, and other materials so they can build up a strong knowledge base. Even young students can gather information by listening to books and viewing videos. Once they have an understanding of their topic they can begin to share what they know by writing with your guidance.

Opinion/Argument

Opinion writing requires taking a particular stance and writing in a way that can persuade others to agree with you. Part of writing an opinion piece is based on knowing enough about the topic to provide facts while trying to get others to see your point of view. Sometimes thought to be reserved for adults, students, for instance, might write essays trying to

Writing Narratives

Narratives can include narratives about personal experiences or fictional stories. Narrative structures typically include a sequence of events, a conflict and resolution, and clear characters and settings.

Writing Informational Texts

Informational texts are designed to be informative and factual and structured to provide detailed information about specific topics.

Writing Opinion Texts

Opinion writing requires taking a particular stance and trying to persuade others to agree with you.

persuade the school cafeteria to provide ice cream to students or to have a pajama day. The point of guiding students as they write opinion pieces is to demonstrate the structure of an argument: Helping students see how to have a main point and then to back up that point with clear ideas.

Overall, guiding students in each type of writing depends on your understanding of how each type of writing is structured and how to break each into steps for your student.

Stages of the Writing Process

Prewriting

Along with the types of writing, it is important to understand the stages in the writing process. When you tutor you will keep both of these aspects of writing in mind as you guide your student. Each type of writing is approached by using the process that real writers go through. The stages in the writing process: (1) prewriting, (2) drafting, (3) revising, (4) editing, and (5) publishing. All of these stages should be taught to your students and you should focus on the stages they need to develop. This may vary depending on the type of writing.

All writers take time to think about their writing before they put pen to paper. There are many ways to guide students as they prepare to write. Some students need to talk through their ideas, others may need to draw pictures, and some may need to write notes or make lists. Prewriting is unique not only to the student but also to the type of writing you are asking them to do. As the tutor, you must be very sure what you want to see from your student so as to guide him or her well. Ongoing assessment is critical.

Drafting

Drafting is the most commonly used stage in the writing process. Most students write according to the directions they are given. In some cases, this step is the only writing stage that students experience. In guided writing the drafting stage is guided by you as the student writes. Since the student has already engaged in prewriting, the drafting should be a fairly easy step. Students may stop and start at times, and it is your role to keep them going and to let them know that in the drafting stage they do not have to write perfectly. The next stages will provide students with time to revise and edit. The goal of drafting is to get ideas on paper and to write quickly and fluently.
Observing students draft is important. You should see students writing easily, and if they are not you want to step in and discuss their ideas with them. Guiding them at key points when they hesitate is important to help them draft.

Prompting students just enough to keep them writing takes time to develop. You have to observe closely and not interrupt the student when the learner is writing and then be prepared to step in when assistance is needed. Most students either draft quickly and easily or they stop and start and worry over spelling and sentence structure. Therefore, it is important to let students know that those aspects of writing will come during the next steps of revising and editing.

Revising

Revising is the next stage of writing. The key to guiding students as they revise their writing is to plan what you want them to focus on changing in their draft. Revision is not editing spelling or correcting grammar; it is focused on the larger ideas in the draft. Students must be guided to reread their drafts and check for clarity and completeness of ideas. Your role is to prompt them to look for these areas in their writing and pose questions that help them see their work in relation to specific aspects of the type of writing they are doing.

Revising

Revising drafts is focused on adding ideas, making changes in organizing ideas, and elaborating on ideas.

When you tutor, you are always looking ahead to where the student's draft should end up. Knowing what you want students to do is important as you guide them along the way. If a student is writing a narrative and includes only one event in the story, as the student revises you need to prompt the learner to read for the sequence of events and check the work to determine whether more should be added to the writing. If the student is writing an informational text and has only one fact detailed, you may need to review the student's prewriting ideas and have him or her add more ideas. Knowing what students need to do during revision is your role and you should be prepared to move them through the revision stage with detailed guidance. Making sure students feel confident as they revise is important. You do not want them to think their draft was incorrect; you want them to know that writing always requires revision.

Editing

Editing writing takes the revised work and goes over each word and sentence to ensure there are no misspelled words, incorrect or missing punctuation, or grammatical mistakes. This can be a daunting task for young students who will not be able to catch all of their errors. Your support as a tutor is critical here as you help students recognize their editing needs without making them feel as though they cannot write. Often you can use aids such as spellcheck, dictionaries, or other texts to help students correct and edit. Editing should only be done if the writing is going to be published. Not all writing pieces need to be published. You should save editing for those works the student wants to share with others and that others will read.

Editing

Editing includes checking the writing for spelling, punctuation, and grammar.

Once you have decided to edit a piece of writing, you should determine how much you want the student to attempt on his or her own and where you will step in to provide input. Having students hold the pen and correct their own work is very important. Taking a pen and marking up students' written works can be demoralizing and make them unsure of their writing abilities. You want to allow students to search for words they are not sure about, have them circle those words, reread their sentences, and place periods where they pause or where it is appropriate. After students have done what they can as you observe and ask questions, you may decide to point out additional editing needs and move to teaching new spelling patterns or punctuation marks. Editing and any type of writing instruction is tied closely to teaching new and needed information. When this is done during guided writing it can be a natural part of discussing writing. Editing is an important part of your writing instruction and can be a powerful part of your lesson. Take care to attend to student confidence and realistic goals for your student based on your observations and assessments.

Publishing

Publishing a student's writing is the final stage of the writing process. Publication involves finding a mode to polish and present a piece of writing. The most common type of publication is to move the text into a printed book. You may also have a student make a PowerPoint booklet or a digital story using videos. In your tutoring you should find a balance between drafting pieces and finding pieces that are important for students to take to the publication stage. Selecting a variety of types of writing is important, as is student motivation. The more motivated students are to write, the more they will want to work through all of the writing stages so they can share their work with an audience. You want to find out what motivates your student. Does he or she like to write for the family? Friends? Build on this knowledge and seek out various ways for your student to publish his or her work.

> *Publishing*
>
> Publishing a student's writing is the final stage of the writing process.
> Publication involves finding a mode to polish and present a piece
> of writing.

Many students do not like to write. They may be used to having to write for school and find it tedious and difficult. Real writers write with their audience in mind. They have a purpose for writing. It is your job during guided writing to help your students find an audience to write for and to motivate them. Writing should be expressive and have meaning for students.

Please view the video for an example of an emergent writer using process writing.

Video 9.2

Teaching Guided Writing

The following section focuses on five areas of teacher knowledge related to guiding writing for students. Each area is divided into three levels: beginner, intermediate, and advanced. As you progress with your understanding of writing instruction you can refer to the different levels to increase your learning.

Guided Writing Content Knowledge

Guiding writing content knowledge is focused on understanding the components of the essential elements of writing processes and types of writing.

1. Knowing student's writing abilities (relying on prior assessments).

2. Understanding the developmental levels of writing.

3. Understanding the various types of writing (narrative, informational, opinion).

4. Understanding the stages of process writing.

Table 9.1 provides an overview of the areas covered in this section.

Table 9.1

Essential Elements	Description
Writing level	Determined by measuring: • oral language, • spelling, and • fluency. Writing abilities change over time. Frequent assessment using oral language assessments, spelling inventories, and observation is key to making sure you know the writing ability of your student. Writing skills vary according to type of writing and knowledge of phonics and spelling patterns. Multiple assessments should be used to determine student's writing needs.
Developmental levels of writing and spelling	All writers are continuing to develop their skills, in elementary instruction, developmental writing levels focus on oral language patterns, spelling, and fluency. Understanding where students developmental levels are is key to planning lessons so they can continue to make progress in these areas. Writing activities should include a variety of genres (e.g., narrative, informational) with extensive modeling.

Essential Elements	Description
Types of writing for elementary students	There are three types of writing used in elementary instruction: • *Narrative:* personal narratives, fiction • *Explanatory/Informational:* nonfiction, reports, newspaper articles • *Argument/Opinion:* thesis, persuasive writing Each type of writing has a unique style and purpose. It is important to know how each type is organized, what type of information is required, and what vocabulary is used and why. Understanding the aspects of each type is required before teaching students how to write each genre.
Process writing stages	There are sequential stages of process writing: • Prewriting • Drafting • Revision • Editing • Publishing

Guided Writing Pedagogical Content Knowledge

Guided writing pedagogical content knowledge is focused on the ways guided writing is taught.

Table 9.2 Guided Writing Pedagogical Content Knowledge

Essential Elements	Description
Writing level	Writer developmental levels determine how you will approach your instruction.
Developmental levels of writing and spelling	Select a writing task that your writer cannot complete on his or her own. Be familiar with the developmental level expected skills.
Types of writing for elementary students	Understand the types of writing and what makes them difficult for your student. Be prepared to step in when necessary to model and explain.
Process writing stages	Understand the stages and what students should be able to do during each stage. Use materials at each stage to provide examples for students. Ask questions as students write to make sure they are on track. Have students stop often to reread their writing aloud.

Guided Writing Curricular Knowledge

Guided writing curricular knowledge is focused on the curricular materials associated with guided writing and their use.

Table 9.3 Guided Writing Curricular Knowledge

Essential Elements	Description
Writing level	Writing levels are not specifically indicated in most lesson materials. Standards and student skills may be listed but there are no prepared activities due to the nature of writing and the need to let students produce ideas. There are examples of writing products to view and adapt to your student.
Developmental levels of writing and spelling	Using the writing process and the types of writing requires modifying tasks to your student's developmental level. There is no set curriculum but there are writing standards by grade level to guide you.
Types of writing for elementary students	Instructional manuals and prompt sheets do exist and can help you break down the steps in process writing as it relates to the different types of writing. Using too many preset activities can result in making students do worksheets. It is best to allow students to come up with writing ideas as you help them; it keeps them interested.
Process writing stages	Each stage of writing has various checklists and peer review activities provided by assessments.

Planning for Guided Writing

Planning for guided writing is complex and involves understanding the writing process and the types of writing. This section is devoted to providing you with sample lesson plan configurations at the beginning, intermediate, and advanced levels based on your understanding of guided writing. Each lesson sample and its accompanying template is designed to provide a framework for organizing your instruction.

Beginner Lesson Plan: Guided Writing

If you are just beginning to tutor, you will want to focus on making sure you are covering the basics of guided writing. The lesson plan format that follows lays out a basic guided writing lesson and can be adapted and used with any stage of the writing process or any type of writing. Italicized text indicates how you should implement the activity.

Table 9.4 Beginner Lesson Plan: Guided Writing

Lesson Component	Purpose	Materials	Implementation		Observations/ Assessments
Guided writing Drafting 10 minutes	To guide writing for students	Paper and marker or computer	Prewriting discussion	*State the purpose of the writing task. Provide an example of the type of writing. Let the student talk about the topic.*	What does the student know about the type of writing?
			Decision about text to be written	*Discuss the ideas in detail and assist the student with deciding exactly what to write.*	How is the student's oral expression of ideas?
			Drafting	*Encourage the student to write and step in with questions and praise as they draft.*	How fluent is the student as he or she writes?
			Rereading	*Have the reader reread the text he or she wrote.*	Was the student able to read the text?

Intermediate Lesson Plan: Guided Writing

As you become more comfortable with using guided writing, you will want to refine your teaching. The lesson plan that follows adds more options for your lesson.

Table 9.5 Intermediate Lesson Plan: Guided Writing

Lesson Component	Purpose	Materials	Implementation		Observations/ Assessments
Guided writing Drafting to revision 10–15 minutes over several sessions	To guide writing for students	Paper and marker or computer	Prewriting discussion	*State the purpose of the writing task. Show a model of the type of writing you want the student to write. Guide the student as he or she talks about the topic to make sure the learner is on track.*	Does the student know enough about the topic to be able to write? Does the student need support with ideas before writing? Is the student able to remember his or her

Decision about text to be written	*Discuss the ideas in detail with the student by having the learner take notes, draw a picture, or make a graphic organizer. Assist the student with deciding exactly what to write.*	sentences during dictation or forgets or changes them? Is the student writing fluently? Is the student able to read his or her words? Can the student evaluate his or her writing ideas?
Drafting	*Observe the student as he or she writes, commenting and prompting as the learner works.*	
Revision	*Have the student reread his or her writing and select two teaching points for the learner to add or change in the paper.*	
Genre check	*Ask the writer to read his or her writing. Ask the writer whether his or her writing structure is similar to the example.*	
Rereading	*Have the writer reread the text he or she wrote. Ask the student whether his or her text is similar to the example text and guide the learner as he or she makes changes.*	

Advanced Lesson Plan: Guided Writing

Once you become advanced in your tutoring, you will want to deepen your instruction. The following lesson plan template provides more challenging teaching ideas for you to use.

Table 9.6

Lesson Component	Purpose	Materials	Implementation		Observations/ Assessments
Guided writing: prewriting to publication 10–15 minutes over several sessions	To guide writing for students	Paper and marker or computer	Prewriting discussion	*State the purpose of the writing task. Show a model of the type of writing you want the student to write. Let the student talk about the topic. Guide the student's ideas by modeling using a prewriting strategy (listing, graphic organizer).*	Does the student know enough about the topic to be able to write? Does the student need support with ideas before writing? Is the student able to follow the example text? Is the student writing fluently? Is the student able to read and evaluate his or her work? Can the student evaluate his or her writing ideas? Can the student evaluate his or her writing in relation to the type of writing? What did the student notice as he or she revised the work? What should be taught next time?
			Decision about text to be written	*Discuss the ideas in detail with the student. Assist the student with deciding exactly what to write, providing guidance to the correct type.*	
			Drafting	*Observe the student as he or she writes. Prompt and praise the student's work, keeping the learner on track with his or her ideas.*	
			Revision	*Focus on a few areas and have the student add text or change the text.*	
			Rereading	*Have the student reread the text he or she wrote. Ask the writer to read his or her writing and compare it with the sample. Ask the reader whether his or her writing makes sense.*	
			Editing	*Assist students in locating spelling, punctuation, and grammatical mistakes.*	
			Publication	*Decide on a mode of publication (typing, PowerPoint, video).*	

These lesson plan samples are intended to assist you as you develop your teaching skills. They move from the simplest type of lesson to much more complex plans.

Summary

Guiding students' writing is designed to help them learn how to improve their writing using the stages of process writing and relying on examples of various types of texts. You play an important role in their development and with careful observation and planning you can teach them how to write different texts, evaluate their own work, and share their work with others. Please review your initial answers and revise your work adding in what you learned.

Pre-Reading Questions

How are student's developmental levels related to teaching guided writing?
Why is it important to teach different types of writing to students?
How can you support students who do not want to revise their work?

Chapter 10: Teaching Writing
Writing Independently

Imagine entering a tutoring room and hearing a struggling adolescent reader/writer reading his story aloud to a small, attentive audience. The young man, an English learner, holds his audience captive as his voice rings out clear and loud while he reads the story he wrote and illustrated over the past several weeks. The audience consists of family members and the university tutor who has guided the youth through the process of writing his story. As he finishes reading, the audience enthusiastically claps and the mother bursts into tears with the realization this was the first complete story her son had written independently, "published," and shared with an audience. The young author looks up with a fantastic smile on his face and rushes to hug his mother who is bursting with pride. This is just one of the many images that emerge from students' participation in independent writing and "author's chair" experiences.

Purpose of the Chapter

This chapter is designed to illustrate the importance of independent writing and to describe the various types of writing produced. Famous children's book authors often talk about how the independent writing process starts for them. Some authors brainstorm ideas. Others doodle, draw, and write words, and some write one word and create a story around a single word. Sharing how successful authors write and produce text can motivate students to try new techniques and writing genres. Most authors when asked what advice they would give a novice writer would say, "Write, write, and write some more." Students, as with authors, get better at writing by writing! They should also be encouraged to explore writing genres and use various writing formats to model their writing, such as using a mentor text to tell their story. Musicians, similar to writers, practice daily to become better at playing their instruments. For musicians to develop their skills they not only need to practice but must also expand their musical repertoire and play different types of music. Writers must do the same thing. Encourage your student to expand his or her writing skills by writing in different genres and formats. Students can begin by writing about what they know best—themselves. Each student has a story to tell and by creating an identity text about some aspect of their life they can share this story with others. Once a child has written a story, he or she can then "publish" the story and share sections of it with others through the author's chair activity. Before you read this chapter, please take a moment to answer the pre-reading questions below. Record your answers so when you are done reading you can go back and review what you have learned.

Pre-Reading Questions

Why should students write on their own?

What does it mean to assist students as they write independently?

In this chapter, more information on the key terms, mentor text, identity text, and author's chair will be provided.

Key Terms

Mentor Text   Author's Chair   Identity Text

Why Is Independent Writing Important?

Just as independent reading is important in improving a student's reading ability, independent writing is integral to assisting writers in becoming proficient and prolific writers. Writing independently does not mean allowing the student to write without support and guidance. Writing independently means students are ready to write on their own after the writing process and strategies for writing have been taught through modeled and shared writing, and rehearsed under a supportive and watchful eye in guided writing. Some students are eager to write independently and have many ideas they want to expand and write about, while others may be a bit more reticent to begin. For students who need more help and support getting started with writing, have them look at some of the shared writing pieces you have worked on together to see if they can glean ideas for their own writing. Brainstorming ideas together and creating a list of topics that might interest them can also provide the support they need to get started. Independent writing can also be assigned after a read aloud or shared reading experience.

Using the Read Aloud Experience to Write Independently

After engaging in a read aloud or interactive read aloud with your student, discuss the parts of the story he or she found engaging. Allow the student to make connections to the text and the story (or literary) elements. Were the characters familiar or funny or different in some way? If so, the student can expand on the character's story by creating a new setting or situation in which to place the character. Remember, literary elements include characterization, setting, theme, mood, plot, and style, which also includes tone and language. Allow your student to peruse the book to look at words and story grammar as he or she begins to write an extension of the story. Using read alouds to extend literary elements allows students to write independently yet still have some needed textual support. Another writing activity offering support is writing independently after a shared reading experience.

Using the Shared Reading Experience to Write Independently

In shared reading, the student engages in reading the text with the tutor. The text may be read and revisited several times so the student has experienced the language from the text often. This reiterative practice with the text allows the student to have more facility with the language. To extend a shared reading to an independent writing activity, students can take the poem or text read during shared reading and expand it, change the text to a readers' theater, or modify it in some way (Swartz, Shook, & Klein, 2002). Adapting text from a read aloud and shared reading involves expanding, adding to the text, or focusing on a specific literary element to create a new story. Using mentor texts as models can also motivate and inspire students to write independently.

Please view the video of a shared writing lesson.

Video 10.1

Using Mentor Text to Write Independently

Mentor texts are published text in all genres that you can use to point out how the author crafted the story (literary elements) or used story grammar or text structure in a particular way so the student can use it as a model to write something similar.

Using mentor texts is an excellent way to get reluctant writers motivated or writers who are just "stuck" on what to write and how to write it "unstuck." While picture books have been used most often as models for mentor texts, informational literature is an excellent genre to use as well. Using informational texts and pointing out the different structures used to create the text—such as cause and effect, problem and solution, description, compare and contrast, and sequencing—provides a great scaffold for students to write in a similar way and to gain a deeper understanding of how the text structure supports the information. Using informational text as mentor text is great for all students but especially for English learners (ELs) who are becoming familiar with English story grammar and text structures. While mentor text can provide support for struggling writers and ELs who

> **Mentor Text**
>
> Mentor texts are usually written texts—but can also be multimodal—that students can use as a model for their writing.

are learning the English language, writing identity texts can be a good way to motivate a student to write independently.

Please view the video of a mentor text writing lesson.

Video 10.2

Using Identity Text to Write Independently

Writing an identity text allows students to position themselves as relevant sources of story knowledge through the creation of a text that is personal and relevant to them.

Identity text, according to Cummins and Early (2011), are written, visual, performed, or produced in other multimodal textual formats, and created by students through their lens, perspective, and voice. Identity text are situated and framed within the student's cultural language and identity. For students from nondominant groups to be successful with literacy, they must also be allowed to contest a single linguistic format and negotiate textual and linguistic understanding through identity text. If a student sees herself or himself in text, sees how the text affects his or her life and can identify with the purpose of the writing activity, the student is then more likely to be engaged in the writing process.

Please view the video of a student writing an identity text.

Video 10.3

How to Assist Students as They Write

In independent writing, students are writing independently but that does not mean they are writing without support or guidance. Support is provided before, during, and after writing. Before beginning independent writing, review a previously taught writing strategy, skill, or genre that the student can either incorporate into his or her writing or use to structure the piece. Also beneficial is reviewing writing genres and formats (writing based on a read aloud, shared reading, mentor text, or identity text) prior to writing so the student can decide how to proceed.

During independent writing, students should have access to writing tools such as a digital or hard copy dictionary, an individual word wall with words related to the student's topic or theme, charts such as expository text structures, a writing genre chart so they can check that their writing is on track, and a block of uninterrupted time. During independent writing, the student should have the opportunity to compose a new story, revise, or edit a piece of writing using what was learned in modeled, guided, and/or shared writing. Since the tutoring is a one-to-one format, it is advantageous to model independent writing and write alongside your student.

After independent writing, it is best to confer with the student. Allow the student to provide details on what she or he wrote and to talk about where the student is headed with the writing piece and any issues, difficulties, questions, or concerns the learner may have about the writing process. It is best to document this information in your anecdotal notes as a reference during each conference. Should your student have similar problems or difficulty with a specific writing issue you can then go back to your notes and remind the student how he or she tackled that issue previously. In this way you are reinforcing the student's understanding of how to make adjustments when the learner gets "stuck" in writing and becomes less dependent on your assistance during conferencing. An example of this could be the student having an issue with his or her compare-and-contrast informational independent writing piece. In a previous conference, you had the student create a Venn diagram and list the items that were both the same and different. This graphic organizer helped the student organize information he or she needed to write the text and made writing independently easier. Remind the student of the previous situation and prompt him or her by saying, "Do you remember what we did last time we needed to organize information in a compare-and-contrast format?" Should the student struggle remembering, you can also show your notes (see Table 10.1) or have the student create his or her own independent writing journal to refer to. Make sure to share your work with your students and talk through issues you may have encountered and any solutions you came up with as you wrote independently. In addition, make sure to have your student set goals for the next independent writing time.

Table 10.1 Example of Anecdotal Independent Writing Notes

Anecdotal Independent Writing Notes		
Date	Observations/Strategies	Goal for Next Writing Lesson
	Student had difficulty writing compare-and-contrast story. A Venn diagram was modeled and the student filled out the information to help organize the text. Topic: 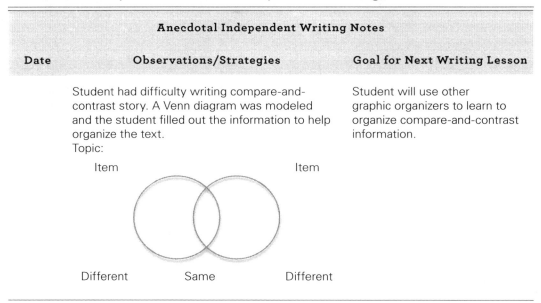	Student will use other graphic organizers to learn to organize compare-and-contrast information.

Completing a writing piece through participation in author's chair represents a wonderful way for the student to not only share his or her work but to also hear the learner's words aloud and have an audience listen and react to the piece. For more information on modeled writing, refer to Chapter 7.

ELs Writing Independently

During each tutoring session ELs should have the opportunity to write independently. Do not assume that their oral language skill is indicative of their writing skill. Many ELs are able to put down on paper what they may have difficulty saying orally. Some ELs are hesitant to pronounce certain words but are very capable of writing these same words down on paper. Make sure you have provided writing support prior to independent writing through modeled minilessons that focus on writing conventions, structures, patterns and the writing process. During independent writing make sure to provide individual word walls, high frequency word lists, sentence frames, or other writing supports that are appropriate for the specific writing genre. Also make sure to expose your EL student to a variety of writing genres. All students should have the opportunity to write independently across genres. Some students may feel comfortable only writing personal narratives so it is important to guide them through the process of understanding how to write informational or opinion/persuasive pieces.

Please view the video of an EL writing independently.

Video 10.4

Author's Chair

Participating in author's chair is a wonderful way to celebrate the young author's writing achievement and hard work. To participate the student has the opportunity to sit in a chair surrounded by tutors and peers and share his or her work. While the process at first seems daunting for the young author, the applause and encouraging comments usually make the activity well worth a few minutes of nervousness.

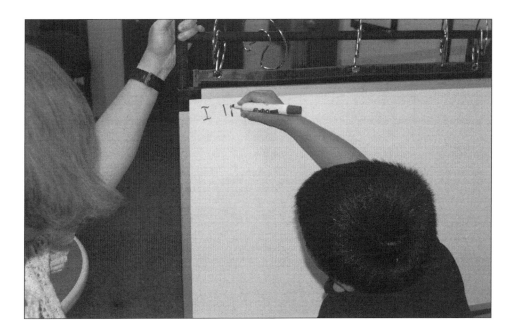

Make time for independent writing during each tutoring lesson. Remember the more the student writes the better at writing she or he will become. Have your students think as an author and remind them that successful authors write every day. The following essential elements will help you prepare for an independent writing lesson.

Essential Elements of Independent Writing

1. Set a purpose for independent writing.

2. Help students expand their writing repertoires (using different genres and formats).

3. Model independent writing behaviors (before, during, and after).

4. Set goals for each independent writing session.

Knowing the steps involved in preparing for any literacy activity is important. Preparation is the key to a successful tutoring experience for both you and your student. There are specific steps to implementing an independent writing lesson.

Teaching and Planning for Independent Writing Behaviors: Tutor Levels

The following section looks at independent writing as it pertains to content, pedagogical, and curricular teacher knowledge (see Chapter 1 for more details). Each area is divided into beginner, intermediate, and advanced. As you develop your understanding of the essential elements in independent writing you can refer to the different sections to increase your understanding.

Independent Writing Content Knowledge

Modeling independent writing content knowledge is based on understanding the essential elements involved in the process of writing independently.

1. Knowing how to set a purpose for independent writing.

2. Being able to select different genres of writing.

3. Understanding how to model independent writing behaviors.

4. Knowing how to assist your student in setting goals for independent writing.

Table 10.2 provides an overview of the areas covered in this section.

Table 10.2

Essential Elements	Description
Set a purpose for independent writing	Know your student's writing level as determined by oral language fluency (recognizing that ELs writing skills may be more developed than their oral language skills), word recognition, and spelling assessments. Set a purpose for independent writing (which part of the writing process will the student engage in).
Genre and writing formats	Have students select a specific genre and make sure to have them explore other genres.
Different independent writing behaviors	Model independent writing behaviors (before, during, and after). Write side-by-side.
Setting goals for independent writing	Set goals for each writing lesson. Assist students in setting their own goals for independent writing.

Independent Writing Pedagogical Content Knowledge

Independent writing pedagogical content knowledge is focused on the ways independent writing is taught.

Table 10.3 Independent Writing Pedagogical Content Knowledge

Essential Elements	Description
Set a purpose for independent writing	The student's independent writing experience and ability will assist you in planning instruction.
Genre and writing formats	Guide the student's selection of a specific genre and text format for independent writing.
Different independent writing behaviors	Understand the independent writing behaviors your student exhibits and the behaviors you need to model.
Setting goals for independent writing	Assist students in setting goals for independent writing. Model before, during, and after writing behaviors.

Independent Writing Curricular Content Knowledge

Independent writing curricular knowledge is focused on the curricular materials associated with independent writing.

Table 10.4 Independent Writing Curricular Content Knowledge

Essential Elements	Description
Independent writing levels	Independent writing levels are individualized and will not be indicated in curricular materials.
Genre and writing formats	Some writing programs include examples of different genres that can be used as a model for independent writing. It is best to find examples of writing genres and formats that are of interest to the student.
Different independent writing behaviors	Specific independent reading behaviors may or may not be cited in curricular materials.
Setting goals for independent writing	Curricular materials may have established goals for the reading materials available in the curriculum but it is best to establish individual goals for your student.

Planning for Independent Writing

Planning for independent writing involves understanding your student's writing skills and interests, writing behaviors, and knowledge of different genres of writing. This section provides you with sample lesson plans at the beginning, intermediate, and advanced levels based on your understanding of independent writing behaviors. Each lesson sample and its accompanying template is designed to provide a framework for organizing your instruction.

Table 10.5 Beginner Lesson Plan: Independent Writing (Based on Read Aloud or Shared Reading)

Lesson Component	Purpose	Materials	Implementation		Observations/ Assessments
Independent writing 10 minutes	To promote independent writing behaviors and strategies in students.	Read aloud or shared reading text	Before reading	Set a purpose for writing. Discuss the literary element or story grammar the student will focus on to write independently. Provide examples from the text to highlight literary element or story grammar. If working with ELs provide sentence frames, individual word walls or other appropriate resources.	Observe student's writing behaviors. Conference Anecdotal notes Set goals for next independent writing period.
			During reading	Provide literary element or story grammar chart. Make sure word wall is available. Take anecdotal notes.	
			After reading	Conference to review writing. Allow student to make comments and talk about his or her writing.	

Table 10.6 Intermediate Lesson Plan: Independent Writing

Lesson Component	Purpose	Materials	Implementation		Observations/ Assessments
Independent writing 10 minutes	To promote independent writing behaviors and strategies in students.	Provide mentor text student has read or heard before.	Before reading	Review the mentor text. Review the structure of the text student will use to create his or her independent writing piece. Review a strategy student can use during writing.	Observe student's writing behaviors. Conference Anecdotal notes Set goals for next independent writing period.
			During reading	Provide word wall. Make mentor text available.	
			After reading	Conference Take anecdotal notes. Allow student to make comments and talk about his or her writing.	

Table 10.7 Advanced Lesson Plan: Independent Writing

Lesson Component	Purpose	Materials	Implementation		Observations/ Assessments
Independent writing 10 minutes	To promote independent writing behaviors and strategies in students.	Informational mentor text	Before writing	Remind student to use focused strategies or to recall minilessons taught.	Observe how student attends to the text structures in nonfiction texts during independent writing time. Set goals for next independent writing period.
			During writing	Provide informational text structure chart. Provide word wall. Make mentor text available.	
			After writing	Conference Take anecdotal notes. Allow student to make comments and talk about his or her writing. Discuss text structure use.	

Summary

These simple lesson plan samples are intended to assist you as you develop your teaching practice. The lessons are developed to provide lesson ideas from beginner to advanced levels. Independent writing helps a student practice writing and use strategies previously taught along with providing the student with choice in selecting writing topics and genres. Please review your initial answers and revise to reflect your learning.

> **Pre-Reading Questions**
>
> Why should students know about different writing genres?
> What is the purpose of having students write an identity text? What should you know about your student's abilities as you plan the lesson?

PART V: MEETING THE NEEDS OF STUDENTS

Knowing your students and their families is key to assisting them as they improve their reading and writing. This final section of the book discusses how to get to know student families and how to communicate with them. It also includes case studies to demonstrate how to adapt instruction to individual student needs.

Chapter 11: Ongoing Family Partnerships

It is the last night of tutoring and a cacophony of voices and languages can be heard coming from tutoring rooms drifting lyrically down the corridor. Small children spill into the hallways to gather snacks and scurry back into the rooms to hear stories read and watch readers' theater in action. All the tutoring rooms are filled with adults eager to see their child's literacy skills on display. In one room you can hear a reader's theater written and performed by the children, another room has children sitting in the "author's chair" as they read their original stories, and in yet another room you can hear a conversation in Spanish as families, tutors, and instructors communicate with one another. The scene is electric as excited children show their families what they have learned in concert with their tutors

and instructors. Laugher and clapping can be heard as performances end and children take their bows. As the families and their children exit, tears of joy can be seen on adult faces as appreciative hugs are exchanged and goodbyes until next time are said.

In another setting, a tutor sits after school with a teacher and a family. The tutor shares the digital story the student created on an iPad and they smile as the story plays. The child explains the story to her family with excitement and explains how she did it by herself. The tutor shares assessments and asks the child to read a familiar story. The family is happy to see that their daughter enjoys reading and that she has written her own book. These scenarios demonstrate the importance of making time to share your students' work with their families and teachers if you tutor within a large established program or through a smaller volunteer program in schools or community centers. Inviting parents to participate throughout the tutoring program is an integral part of any student's success.

Purpose of the Chapter

Funds of Knowledge

Funds of knowledge are the types of conventional and nonconventional literacies that students have access to in their household and community.

The purpose of this chapter is to discuss the importance of reaching out to families in your tutoring. Including family members not just in the literacy activities but also as active members of the literacy program provides an enriching experience for all involved stakeholders. There are several ways you can communicate with families and include them in the tutoring process: (1) informal check-in and drop-off conversations, (2) sharing student work, (3) providing brief reports on student progress, and (4) sharing in-depth assessment reports.

Families may come from very diverse social, economic, linguistic, and cultural backgrounds. Understanding the funds of knowledge (Moll, Amanti, Neff, & Gonzalez, 1992) or the types of literacies and texts used in the students' household and community is essential information needed to incorporate into individualized lesson design and development.

Valuing the literacy skills and knowledge of families is crucial to establishing relationships with the student. This chapter will provide details on the different ways you can interact with families and include them in the tutoring process. Before you read the chapter, please take a moment to answer the pre-reading questions that follow. Record your answers so when you are done reading you can go back and review what you have learned.

Pre-Reading Questions

How are families invited to participate in the tutoring experience?

In what ways can we communicate with families sharing the tutoring experience?

What are appropriate methods of communication with families?

A few key terms that will be used throughout the chapter are listed below.

Key Terms

Funds of Knowledge   Confidentiality

Working with Families: The Four Cs

We rely on the four Cs in our approach to tutoring: Care, Communicate, Confidentiality, and Connect. While these ideas may be taken for granted, you want to make sure you understand how to include families in your tutoring as much as possible. As mentioned in Chapter 2, families are the first teachers, and therefore respecting the family's wishes is key to making sure your student is successful. Please note that we use the term *families* rather than parents due to the variety of family structures students may have. Each area will be described in detail below.

Care

Students and families can quickly tell if you truly care about them. If you are going to tutor struggling readers it is very important to make sure you enjoy working with children. We have supervised tutoring programs for a long time and, unfortunately, we do see students who say they want to be teachers and love children and yet when they run into students who struggle with reading and who at times do not want to read or write, they become frustrated. Students in tutoring programs are typically there because they are having trouble. They are not always initially excited to come to tutoring sessions. They may anticipate that they will have to do skill worksheets, read texts that are extremely hard, or be embarrassed. Some of the students may be pulled out of their classroom for tutoring, which can cause them to become self-conscious. Being empathetic, patient, and caring are the most important parts of tutoring. It may mean that if your student is having a bad day, you elect to read to them instead of having them read. Or you modify your lesson to include writing about their favorite topic for that one day rather than a more difficult topic. Basically, you are observing them and providing the time to take their feelings and abilities into account as you teach each time. While we advocate for always trying to complete all the tutoring activities, we also know that a stressed child is one who is not ready to take on challenging tasks. At times, we have also noticed that some tutors become frustrated and tend to blame the child. They make statements such as, "He won't read" or "She is just trying to avoid writing" or inappropriate statements such as, "He's just lazy." These are signs the lesson needs adjusting, not the child. If lessons are planned based on students' developmental levels, interests, each activity is brief and focused, and you are praising their attempts, then most children find tutoring sessions enjoyable. If lessons are not thought out, if the activities are too difficult and take too long, the lesson will not go well. Therefore, we emphasize caring about your student and examining *your* teaching if things are not going well. As teachers, we are in charge of the lesson, the time, and most of all the environment and attitude. It is our responsibility to make sessions enjoyable. This extends to families and how you interact with them.

Communicate

Ongoing positive communication is extremely important. Keeping in communication with the families throughout the tutoring program is important for several reasons. First, the safety of the student is of utmost importance so knowing where you will tutor, who your supervisor is, and who will pick up the student after each session is vital. In each session you should communicate briefly with the parent, caregiver, or teacher. Families will usually take this opportunity to chat informally about tutoring or their child's school experience, giving you the opportunity to get to know more about their child. It is important to be positive and emphasize what the student is doing well by showing writing samples and books read during the session.

Confidentiality

Often families share other issues that may be occurring within the family dynamic. For this reason, you must know that maintaining confidentiality is important.

We must maintain confidentiality and comply with the Family Educational Rights and Privacy Act, or FERPA (http://www2.ed.gov/policy/gen/guid/fpco/ferpa/index.html).

FERPA protects the educational records of students. While family members or teachers may share information with you, you want to make sure you keep the information to yourself. Family members may also share personal information about the family and/or the child. While not covered by FERPA, the information can at times be sensitive so you need to ensure you do not share it with anyone. You, as the tutor, will have the most contact with the family so you want to make sure you are professional.

Whether communication is through traditional means such as electronic access to technology or through email or telephone, connecting with families and keeping them informed helps build lasting relationships. Due to financial circumstances, some families may not have phones nor access to the Internet at home. Meeting with them at each tutoring session at pickup and drop-off is vital to keeping the lines of communication open.

Connect

Making connections between student's lives and your teaching can make a huge difference. You want to encourage families to participate by communicating with them but also by making specific inquiries about how they think their child is doing. Families who speak no or limited English can be as fully engaged as the monolingual English-speaking families. Full engagement from the families helps create a true partnership. Having families interested and fully invested in your tutoring helps keep the students motivated and lowers absenteeism. Ensuring that the student attends all tutoring sessions is beneficial for both the student and the tutor. There are two common ways to connect with families: informal daily visits as discussed in the previous section, and conferences.

Family Conferences

The most beneficial way to communicate with families is to have a family conference. Families are the experts on their children and honoring their knowledge is key. Before you begin any meeting, you will want to listen to their thoughts to see what they consider important in their child's literacy. Once you have spent time listening to the family, you can begin to share your observations and assessments about their child. Each conference should focus on the student's reading levels and their writing abilities. Demonstrating their learning with examples and materials is important, as is making sure the student participates in the meeting. We recommend that you and your student prepare a lesson together to show the family what their child has learned. The student, with your help, also takes responsibility for preparing for the conference. You and the student will, for instance, consult and select activities to share at the conference and together walk the family through the lesson, explaining what was learned and showing the family how the student used word sorts, displaying writing artifacts, or reading sections of a story for author's chair. Groups of students may take part in readers' theater to entertain families while displaying their newly acquired literacy skills. Having an interpreter to assist with translations during the family conference is an excellent way to communicate with parents who do not speak English. There is no set number of conferences, but the more you are able to communicate with families, the more you can adapt your instruction.

Table 11.1 Family Night Guidelines

Welcome

Your Role	Your Student's Role	Materials
Introduce yourself.	Share a positive thing you and the student have done together.	One book (focus on reading) that the student enjoyed.

Smile
Be positive and redirect the conversation if needed.
Say one thing about where you are in your program.
Say one thing your student does really well.

Digital Stories, Identity Text and Other Writing

Your Role	Your Student's Role	Materials
Explain the steps and process involved in making the digital story or identity text and why it is important for your student's growth.	Explain their ideas for the story. Explain the writing process for the piece.	Digital story and/or identity text and writing samples

Include all of the steps in the process.
Share various products.
Share role of spelling in relation to writing.

Guided Reading

Your Role	Your Student's Role	Materials
Explain the purpose of guided reading.	Listen and read text excerpt.	Running records Texts read

Make sure the family understands developmental levels of reading and writing.
Make sure the family understands the role of cueing systems and prompting.

Recommendations

Your Role	Your Student's Role	Materials
Explain two or three recommendations that will assist families in working with their students.	Participate in demonstrating the recommended activities.	Those required for specific recommended activities

Each recommendation MUST come from a research base.
Explain each recommendation slowly and model it.
Include materials the family can actually access at home.
Talk specifically about why your recommendation is helpful.

Open House

If you tutor in a large program, open houses are great ways to connect with families. For many families, this is not just an opportunity to meet the tutors and instructors but to also visit the tutoring site. The open house can be an excellent opportunity for you to prepare a brief introduction about yourself and what you hope to accomplish during the sessions and to communicate this to parents. At this time families should be provided with the opportunity to ask the instructors any questions. Once you have introduced yourself to the child and family, you should explain what will occur during each tutoring session. It is important to show the family the various tools and technology available for tutoring. Families can be expected to ask the tutor specific questions regarding tutoring and will often share any concerns they may have about their child's literacy skills or information regarding allergies or health issues. You can ask the student questions about his or her reading interests to help the student select text for the first tutoring session. You should end the session by thanking the families for coming and express your excitement for the opportunity to work with their child.

Table 11.2

	Agenda for Open House
Welcome	Families are welcomed.
Introductions	Tutoring center instructors are introduced and briefly share their teaching background.
Overview	Families are provided with an interactive overview of the program that details: • Tutoring dates • Tutoring times • Drop-off and pickup location • Attendance policy • Center contact information to notify staff of child's absence • Emergency packets are provided to families

Agenda for Open House	
Questions	Families are encouraged to ask any questions prior to meeting with their child's tutor. Families are thanked for their attendance.
Meet with tutors	Families meet with tutors who have prepared a brief presentation about the tutoring experience. • Tutors introduce themselves to the families. • Tutors briefly explain what will occur during each hour session. • Tutors get to know more about their student and his or her reading interests. • Tutors thank the families for attending. • Tutors remind the student that each will see each other the following week on the specified day.
Center tour and further questions	Families are encouraged to tour the facilities and ask questions prior to leaving.

At the end of the tutoring program families can be invited to a family conference to engage in a literacy celebration.

Assessment Reports

We also recommend providing the families with ongoing reports to share how their child is doing. An example is provided here:

Student Assessment Report

Overview of the Informal Observational Assessments

Overall, Tim reads at approximately a first-grade level. The following report describes the assessments administered during the three-week summer session. The first section describes assessment information and analysis while the second section provides additional information about reading and reading difficulties in general to provide background information and more detailed explanations of your child's current developmental levels in relation to reading and writing.

Report completed by: _____   Date: _____

Table 11.3

Assessment Tools		
Word Recognition	**Comprehension**	**Fluency**
Analytical reading inventory (Woods & Moe, 2011)	Analytical reading inventory (Woods & Moe, 2011)	Analytical reading inventory (Woods & Moe, 2011)
Leveled text reading (Fountas & Pinnell, 1996)	Leveled text reading (Fountas & Pinnell, 1996)	Leveled text reading (Fountas & Pinnell, 1996)

Table 11.4

Reading Assessments		
Analytical reading inventory	An Informal Reading Inventory (IRI) is an authentic standards-based assessment. It is composed of a series of reading passages that begin at preprimer level and progressively become more difficult. As a reader progresses from easier passages to more difficult ones, the examiner records, analyzes, and summarizes data that reflect the reader's application or default of standards and indicators of reading competency: prior knowledge/prediction, word recognition, fluency, and comprehension. Knowing Informal Reading Inventory data enables classroom teachers, reading specialists, and school psychologists to make evidence-based instructional decisions and to report student progress in standards-based terms. Standardized testing does not provide such detailed instructionally connected data (Woods & More, 2011, p. 2).	
ARI Levels: preprimer, primer, and Level 2	**Focus Area**	**Comments**
	Accuracy	• Struggled with *poor* for *paper, learn* for *last, big* for *bag* • Does not chunk or use spelling patterns to sound out words. • Does use first and last letters
	Fluency	• Reads quickly • Some phrasing
	Comprehension	• Could recount some events. • Struggled with details based on errors.
ARI summary and analysis	The ARI assessment is difficult. There are few picture supports and the student has to answer both literal and inferential questions. Tim struggled with the assessment texts. He substituted words based on the first and last letters. These errors did affect his comprehension and fluency at times as he misunderstood some of the detailed comprehension questions. He is a quick reader and likes to read fast, which causes him to skim over unknown words.	

Table 11.5

Leveled text reading	Reading leveled texts is a foundational part of reading instruction in the elementary grades. Different from traditional reading assessments, leveled readers provide picture support, controlled vocabulary, and patterned texts that increase in difficulty at very small intervals. The discrete levels allow for systematic text selection for young readers still acquiring specific reading strategies similar to the levels of sports such as ski runs, karate levels, etc. Students learning to read work with teacher support to slowly increase their reading level.
Running records	Running records are used to analyze student accuracy percentages and strategy use while reading text.

Text:	Focus Area	Comments
Level H	Accuracy	• Substitutes words (e.g., *surprised* for *supposed*) • Some rereading
	Fluency	• Reads quickly • Little expression at times
	Comprehension	• Varied—sometimes able to retell events, sometimes unable to recall story
Text summary and analysis		Tim reads at level H. These texts have pictures and larger amounts of text. Tim uses the first letters of words, quickly substitutes words, and keeps reading. He does not go back to make sure what he read makes sense. Tim does correct himself when prompted to reread. His comprehension varied across all of the texts he read. At times, he could retell the story and at times he made statements that were not connected to the text.
Overall summary of reading observations (ARI and text) and analysis		Tim read texts and the ARI assessment at a first-grade level. Overall, Tim is an early reader (see page 9) and is able to use sight words and the initial letters to approximate words. Tim does substitute incorrect words as he reads and does not reread. He needs to work on self-monitoring by rereading and checking his understanding as he reads.
Developmental reading level		Early reader

Table 11.6 Recommendations

Area	Recommendations
Word recognition	• Reading and stopping to retell the story events to ensure correct reading with supportive strategy prompts. • Encouraging rereading of sentences to check for meaning.

Summary

Inviting parents and families to participate fully in the tutoring program allows for open communication between the tutoring program personnel and the families. Families feel comfortable asking questions and seeking information that will benefit their child and often share this information with other friends and families who are not part of the tutoring program. Our current families help recruit new students to the programs through word of mouth. Review your initial responses and add in any new information you learned.

> **Pre-Reading Questions**
>
> In what ways can families participate in the tutoring program?
>
> Why is it important for families to stay informed about events and activities sponsored by the tutoring center?

Chapter 12: Putting It All Together

Now that you are familiar with the essential elements of literacy instruction and assessment, it is time to apply this knowledge to actual students. This chapter is based on two case studies of students at various reading and writing levels and uses videos to demonstrate the relationship between assessment and instruction. Excellent instruction depends on taking research-based teaching practices and adjusting them to meet the needs and interests of your individual student. Each student brings unique strengths and areas of need. Realizing how to adapt your instruction to them is key, and adapting the instruction depends on ongoing assessment and observations.

Purpose of the Chapter

This chapter is designed to provide you with two video case studies of young readers and writers. Each case is unique and you will be asked to view the videos and reflect on what the tutor planned and how the lesson follows or expands on the plan. While there is no way to create a set recipe for tutoring, there are common practices related to students' levels of reading that will help you. The videos are designed to demonstrate key aspects of teaching reading and writing to learners at various levels. Before you read this chapter, please take a moment to answer the pre-reading questions that follow. Record your answers so when you are done reading you can go back and review what you have learned.

> **Pre-Reading Questions**
>
> What do you know about how to adapt your instruction to meet the needs of particular students?
>
> How can you use your assessments to plan your teaching?

Essential Elements of Tutoring

Tutoring is complex but it is also important to rely on the basics. As you prepare to tutor keep the following in mind:

1. Understanding literacy.

2. Understanding the basic types of reading and writing instruction.

3. Using assessments to determine how to plan instruction.

4. Adapting instruction to meet the needs of your student.

Each essential element of tutoring should guide your instruction. Setting up the tutoring environment is also important. Make sure to have all necessary materials available and ready to go prior to tutoring. Creating an inviting atmosphere is essential. Picture 12.1 demonstrates one way to set up a tutoring table and workspace.

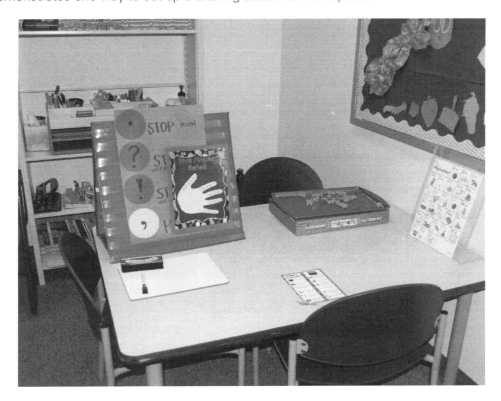

Now that we have covered all major components of the tutoring program we provide you with sample lesson plan templates to guide your work.

Sample Lesson Plans

We have included two sample lesson plan templates with the various areas listed. The first sample is set for a 30-minute lesson but it can be modified for an hour-long session. The four areas: read aloud, guided reading, guided writing, and independent reading are listed. The additional focus area can be used for detailed word study or specific writing tasks. The second sample template is designed for a 60-minute tutoring session.

Table 12.1 Sample Lesson Plan: 30 Minutes

Student Name: _____ **Tutor Name:** _____

Reading Level: _____ **Date:** _____

Read Aloud 5 minutes	Guided Reading 10 minutes	Guided Writing 10 minutes	Independent Reading 5 minutes	Additional Focus Area* 5 minutes
Objectives Student listens and responds to text.	**Objectives** Student reads, uses visual, contextual, and syntactic strategies and responds to text.	**Objectives** Student writes in response to a text or event.	**Objectives** Student reads independent text fluently.	**Objectives** Student ...
Activity	**Activity**	**Activity**	**Activity**	**Activity**
Book title	**Book title**	**Materials** Paper/dry erase board/computer	**Book title**	**Materials**
Description of implementation Prepared questions, sequence of activities, etc.	**Description of implementation** Prepared questions, sequence of activities, etc.	**Description of implementation** Prepared questions, sequence of activities, etc.	**Description of implementation** Prepared questions, sequence of activities, etc.	**Description of implementation** Prepared questions, sequence of activities, etc.
Observation Notes Was the student engaged? How was the student's comprehension?	**Observation Notes** Was the book at the student's level? What were your observations on comprehension and fluency? What strategies did you notice the student use?	**Observation Notes** Was the student writing fluently? Did the student think of ideas easily? How much support was needed?	**Observation Notes** Was the book at the student's level? What were your observations on the student's fluency rate and expression?	**Observation Notes**
Ideas for next lesson How does this affect your next lesson? What will you do in the next lesson? Do you have any concerns or questions?	**Ideas for next lesson** How does this affect your next lesson? What will you do next time? Do you have any concerns or questions?	**Ideas for next lesson** How does this affect your next lesson? What will you do next time? Do you have any concerns or questions?	**Ideas for next lesson** How does this affect your next lesson? What will you do next time? Do you have any concerns or questions?	**Ideas for next lesson** How does this affect your next lesson? What will you do next time? Do you have any concerns or questions?

* The additional focus area for each lesson should be based on your assessments. Typical areas might include letter or word work, additional comprehension study, or digital stories.

Table 12.2 Sample Lesson Plan: 60 Minutes

Lesson Component	Purpose	Materials	Implementation		Observations/ Assessments
Read aloud 15 minutes	Select a purpose for the read aloud based on learning objectives, strategy, or modeling technique to be taught.	Select an informational or nonfiction text.	Before reading	Introduce text with learning objectives as focus. Generate interest in the text. Make sure students understand text features. Preview the text if text structures are new to the students.	Observe how student attends to the text during read aloud. Listen to answers, predictions, questions, and comments from the student. Check retelling for clear understanding of the story structure elements.
			During reading	Create questions to ask during the read aloud that will meet objectives and purpose. Mark appropriate pages with Sticky Notes and questions. Follow up on student's comments.	
			After reading	Engage in activities that extend student's comprehension of the text: e.g., writing for a different purpose and from a different perspective. Use a sentence frame activity. Allow students to make connections to text. Ask student how story relates to him or her.	

Lesson Component	Purpose	Materials	Implementation		Observations/ Assessments
Guided reading 15 minutes	Reader reads, uses visual, contextual, and syntactic strategies and responds to text.	Text	Book introduction	Ask the reader to predict what the text is about based on the title and cover. State the book's main idea in one sentence. Let the reader skim through the pages and share his or her thoughts. Clear up any misconceptions the reader may have. Ask the reader to confirm or reject his or her prediction. Review the strategies the reader should focus on as he or she reads the text.	Was the book at the student's level? What was the student's accuracy rate? How was the student's fluency? Was it consistent throughout the book or varied? What strategies did you notice the reader use? What did your miscue analysis reveal? Did the student understand the text? Was the student's retelling accurate and thorough? Did he or she answer specific questions correctly?
			New word focus	Select one word that the reader may not know. Read the word to the student and explain its meaning. Have the reader find the word in the text and read the word in the sentence. Have the reader construct the word using magnetic letters or write it on a whiteboard.	
			Reading	Support the reader by using prompts when he or she stops at an unknown word. Reinforce and praise when the reader uses appropriate prompts. Anticipate and prompt before or as a student comes across an unknown word to reinforce use of a prompt.	

			Strategy instruction	Review and praise one reading strategy the reader used. Teach a new strategy based on the reading.
			Comprehension check	Ask the reader to retell the events or facts in the text. Ask the reader follow-up questions about details and interpretations of the text.
			Rereading	Explicitly teach and model a key strategy by showing the reader his or her miscue. Have the reader reread the text emphasizing the target strategy.

Lesson Component	Purpose	Materials	Implementation		Observations/ Assessments
Guided writing: prewriting to publication 15 minutes over several sessions	To guide writing for students	Paper and marker or computer/electronic device	Prewriting discussion	State the purpose of the writing task. Show a model of the type of writing you want the student to write. Let the student talk about the topic. Guide the student's ideas by modeling using a prewriting strategy (listing, graphic organizer).	Does the student know enough about the topic to be able to write? Does the student need support with ideas before writing? Is the student able to follow the example text? Is the student writing fluently? Is the student able to read and evaluate his or her work? Can the student evaluate his or her writing ideas? Can the student evaluate his or her writing in relation
			Decision about text to be written	Discuss the ideas in detail with the student. Assist the student with deciding exactly what to write, providing guidance to the correct type.	

Lesson Component	Purpose	Materials	Implementation		Observations/ Assessments
			Drafting	Observe the student as he or she writes. Prompt and praise the student's work, keeping the learner on track with his or her ideas.	to the type of writing? What did the student notice as he or she revised the work? What should be taught next time?
			Revision	Focus on a few areas and have the student add text or change the text.	
			Rereading	Have the student reread the text he or she wrote. Ask the writer to read his or her writing and compare it with the sample. Ask the reader whether his or her writing makes sense.	
			Editing	Assist students in locating spelling, punctuation, and grammatical mistakes.	
			Publication	Decide on a mode of publication (typing, PowerPoint, video).	

Lesson Component	Purpose	Materials	Implementation		Observations/ Assessments
Independent reading 10 minutes	To promote independent reading behaviors and strategies in students.	Self-selected independent level reading material/ book	Before reading	Assist students in the process of self-selecting a nonfiction text at their independent reading level. Review text structures for cause and effect, or problem solution nonfiction text.	Observe how student attends to the text structures in nonfiction texts during independent reading time. Have student provide written details from the story in his or her response journal.
			During reading	Remind the student to apply the comprehen-sion strategies taught in previous lessons to help the learner understand difficult text.	
			After reading	Have student provide a short, written review on the material read in the response journal. Have student share his or her work.	

Lesson Component	Purpose	Materials	Implementation		Observations/ Assessments
Independent writing 5 minutes	To promote independent writing behaviors and strategies in students.	Informational mentor text	Before writing		Observe how student attends to the text structures in nonfiction texts during independent writing time. Set goals for next independent writing period.
			During writing	Provide informational text structure chart. Provide word wall. Make mentor text available.	
			After writing	Conference Take anecdotal notes. Allow student to make comments and talk about his or her writing. Discuss text structure use.	

Reading Case Studies

Case studies can provide examples for how to plan for instruction and document observations for future planning. The case studies are focused on individual students. As you watch the video case studies, make sure you review the lesson plan excerpts as you view the video.

Table 12.3 Reading Case Study 1

Case	Overview
Second Grade Student	Age: 7
	Grade level: Second
	Interests: She loves to read the Don't Let the Pigeon Drive the Bus series by Mo Willems.
	She likes the color pink.
	Her favorite foods: enchiladas, tacos, Chinese food
	Reading Level: Early reader
	Text Level: L
	Spelling Stage: Within word pattern
	Fluency Rate/Qualitative Features:
	Writing Stage: Beginning—Writes several sentences about a topic, spells simple words.
	Reading Strengths and Weakness: Uses picture cues and rereads text for understanding. Retells what she read. Needs to continue working on inferential comprehension.
	Writing Strengths and Weakness: Selects own topic. Writes several sentences about a topic. Spells simple words and high frequency words. Can read own writing. Needs to consistently use conventions (punctuation).

The first video lesson is centered on reading instruction. You will see how the read aloud is described in the lesson plan and how it is implemented with the second grade student. Note the observations and think about how you might make adjustments to the lesson if you were the tutor.

Table 12.4 Reading Case Study Lesson Plan

Reading Lesson Plan for Case Study 1

Lesson Component	Purpose	Materials	Implementation		Observations/ Assessments
Read aloud 15 minutes	CCSS.ELA-LITERACY.RL.2.4 Describe how words and phrases (e.g., regular beats, alliteration, rhymes, repeated lines) supply rhythm and meaning in a story, poem, or song. Student will be able to describe how words and phrases supply rhythm in a poem. I chose this book because she loves poetry and books that rhyme.	*Where the Sidewalk Ends* by Shel Silverstein	Before reading	• Generate interest in the text by introducing the text and the author. • Explain the text feature, poetry. • Preview the text genre as a collection of poems. • Ask the student to listen carefully for language patterns.	The student was able to quickly identify the rhyming words in the text. She understood the ending rime sounds and was able to construct her own rhyming words.
			During reading	• Call attention to rhyming patterns within the poem and ask student to identify rhyming words.	She struggled with creating new ideas to write about.
			After reading	• Extend the student's comprehension of the unique feature of poetry by creating sentences using rhyming words from the poem. • Allow the student to make connections to text by using sentence frames to create new sentences that rhyme. "Let's have one day for _____ where you can make _____."	She needs to work on learning about the various types of poetry and be encouraged to create her own.

Lesson Component	Purpose	Materials	Implementation		Observations/ Assessments
Independent reading

10 minutes | CCSS: CCSS. ELA-LITERACY. RF.2.3 Know and apply grade-level phonics and word-analysis skills in decoding words.

Objective: Student will be able to decode words by applying grade-level phonics and word-analysis skills.

Rationale: I chose this book because it is within her reading level (J) and she enjoys Junie b. Jones so I am hoping she will like this book also.

CCSS: CCSS. ELA-LITERACY. RL.2.7 Use information gained from the illustrations and words in a print or digital text to demonstrate understanding of its characters, setting, or plot.

Objective: Student will be able to demonstrate understanding of the characters, setting, or plot by using information gained from the text. | Independent level reading material/ book Fancy Nancy: Pajama Day | Before reading | • Predict whether this book will be similar to the last Fancy Nancy book we read, and how they may be different.

• Review the vocabulary learned from the first Fancy Nancy book and try to find that vocabulary in this book.

• Introduce the five finger retell as a comprehension tool with a focus on the beginning, middle, end, setting, and characters.

• Use context clues to understand new vocabulary words.

• Compare and contrast with previously read Fancy Nancy story. | The student was able to recognize her previous knowledge of the characters in the series.

The student used her background knowledge and the text predict to define the word "posh".

Student did understand the focus areas of the five finger retell.

Able to comprehend story as she read.

Read fluently on first reading. Did decode and reread to confirm own reading.

Difficult words (spaniel, unique)

Student was able to retell the five aspects of the story in order and recall details.

Added in review with sight word cards of unfamiliar new vocabulary with a focus on meaning:

ecstatic
exhausted
posh
Merci
unique
ensemble
spectacular |
| | | | During reading | | |
| | | | After reading | | |

Lesson Component	Purpose	Materials	Implementation		Observations/ Assessments
Guided reading 15 minutes	CCSS: CCSS.ELA-LITERACY. RL.2.1 Ask and answer such questions as who, what, where, when, why, and how to demonstrate understanding of key details in a text. Objectives/ Rationale: Student will be able to demonstrate understanding of key details in a text by retelling the story including who, what, where, when, and why. I chose this book because it is within her instructional reading level (J).	Sam and the Firefly by P. D. Eastman, Level J	Book introduction	Ask the reader to predict what the text is about based on the title and cover. Let the reader skim through the pages and share his or her thoughts. Ask the reader to confirm or reject his or her prediction. Our focus will be to read the conversation fluently, as it would be a conversation between us. We will continue to focus on pausing at punctuation.	Student was able to predict what the story was about "A firefly?" Did ask about what a firefly was, introduced firefly. Prompted to read fluently.
			New word focus	Select one word that the reader may not know. Hoo" Read the word to the student and explain its meaning. Have the reader find the word in the text and read the word in the sentence.	Taught the word "who" versus "Hoo" Student was able to read fluently and with expression.
			Reading	Support the reader by using prompts when he or she stops at an unknown word. Reinforce and praise when the reader uses appropriate prompts. Anticipate and prompt before or as a student comes across an unknown word to reinforce use of a prompt.	Did begin to skip words in her efforts to read fluently, able to self-correct with some prompting and maintain expression.
			Strategy instruction	Review and reinforce fluency. Teach a new strategy based on the reading.	Student was able to respond correctly to during reading comprehension checks, both recall and inferential.
			Comprehension check	Ask the reader to retell the events or facts in the text. Ask the reader follow-up questions about details and interpretations of the text.	
			Rereading	Explicitly teach and model a key strategy by showing the reader his or her miscue. Have the reader reread the text emphasizing the target strategy.	Student maintained expressive fluent reading throughout the text.

Now that you have reviewed the lesson plan, please view video 12.1.

Video 12.1

The second case study is focused on how to teach writing. It includes a read aloud designed to provide a poetry model for the student, followed by a lesson on how to write poetry. Notice how the tutor makes adjustments to the student as they complete the activities.

Table 12.5 Writing Case Study 2

Case	Overview
Fifth-Grade Student	Age: 10
	Grade level: Fifth
	Interests: Drawing, writing poetry, soccer, basketball. Loves cheese pizza and the color pink.
	Reading Level: Transitional/level 5 instructional in ARI Text Level: U
	Spelling Stage: Late within word pattern
	Fluency Rate/Qualitative features:
	Writing Stage: Conventional writing—Bridging on the writing continuum.
	Reading Strengths and Weakness: Enthusiasm for reading/higher level comprehension.
	Writing Strengths and Weakness: Enjoys writing/spelling and punctuation.

Table 12.6 Writing Case Study Lesson Plan

Writing Lesson Plan for Case Study 2

Lesson Component	Purpose	Materials	Implementation		Observations/ Assess-ments
Read aloud 20 minutes	CCSS.ELA-LITER-ACY.RL.5.4 Determine the meaning of words and phrases as they are used in a text, including figurative language such as metaphors and similes. Objective 1: Student will be able to break a part a poem to find meaning. Objective 2: Student will be able to figure out the meaning of metaphors and similes. Objective 3: Student will be able to figure out a meaning of a word based on how it was used in a text. The student has been asking to do more poetry and after evaluating my video, I realized my read alouds were too long. So, a poem would be perfect to keep her attention, and it is also something she has been asking about. Plus, we have done nonfiction and fiction, so it would be good to introduce another writing genre.	Raindrop Shape poem	Before reading	I will introduce the poem "Raindrop." This is called a shape poem, because it is in a shape of an object. Usually the shape has to do with the topic of the poem.	The student has mastered objective 1–3 if she can break the pieces of the poem apart and find a deeper meaning within the poem. I will know if she mastered this objective if she is able to participate in the poetry discussion and can bring out her meanings of the poem.
			During reading	Then I will read the poem aloud to her.	She wanted to read along. Read fluently.
			After reading	We will begin going line by line to find meaning within the poem.	Discussed favorite parts of the poem. She reread the lines she liked.
					She connected the poem to her own experiences.
				After I read the poem I will have the student do a quick write about what the poem was able and what she wants to discuss.	

Table 12.7

Lesson Component	Purpose	Materials	Implementation		Observations/Assess-ments
Guided writing: prewriting to publica-tion Writing a Shape Poem 15 minutes over several sessions	CCSS. ELA-LITERA-CY.W.5.3.D Use concrete words and phrases and sensory details to convey experiences and events precisely. Student will be able to create her poem by using details that focus on the student's sensory experiences. Along with reading poetry, the student has also been wanting to write more poetry. This seemed like a good, simple way to create a poem out of the painting color cards.	Paper and marker	Prewriting discussion	After my read aloud, we will quickly discuss what happened within the text (a mini-discussion). Then I will show the student examples of other types of shape poems. We will then brainstorm and create our own by picking a shape we want to write a poem about.	The student was able to come up with a topic on her own. Began by planning 6 lines.
			Decision about text to be written	Student will be able to put together a color poem that focuses on the senses to describe how a color looks, feels, smells, and tastes.	She Is the student writing fluently? The student was able to create a poem using a simile.
			Drafting	Student will be able to draft her own ideas.	Can the student evaluate his or her writing ideas?
			Revision	Focus on simile and have the student add text or change the text.	The student was able to evaluate her writing in relation to the use of description.
			Rereading	Have the student reread the text she wrote. Ask the writer to read his or her writing and compare it with the sample. Ask the reader whether his or her writing makes sense.	"The cat is like a lion." The student was comfort-able during the revising and editing stages.
			Editing	Assist students in locating spelling, punctuation, and grammatical mistakes.	What did the student notice as he or she revised the work?
			Publication	Decide on a mode of publication (typing, PowerPoint, video).	

Now that you have reviewed the lesson plan, please view video 12.2.

Video 12.2

Both of these lessons were planned with care prior to the lesson. The tutors were prepared with their purpose and their objectives for their students based on previous observations and assessments. The tutors were true to their lessons, but they were able to make small adjustments as they worked with each young student. Planning lessons and being prepared is one of the most important elements of tutoring. Once you have laid the groundwork and thought through your lesson, you can allow your teaching to be responsive to student motivations, interests, and abilities. Tutoring should be enjoyable for you and your student; they should feel supported as they work on their literacy development. The most important aspect of tutoring to remember is to smile and appreciate your student so you can support their learning.

Summary

All of the instructional methods we have reviewed should be familiar to you now. Relying on the essential elements as you plan and teach will provide you with a basic starting place. Once you become comfortable with the essential elements of tutoring and with your students, you can begin to modify your lessons to better meet their needs.

REFERENCES

Adams, M. J. (1990). *Beginning to Read: Thinking and Learning about Print.* Cambridge, MA: MIT Press.

Anderson, R. C., Hiebert, E. H., Scott, J. A., & Wilkinson, I. A. G. (1985). *Becoming a nation of readers: The report of the Commission on Reading.* Washington, DC: The National Institute of Education.

Andrew, T. (2105). *Trombone Shorty.* New York, NY: Harry Abrams.

Atwell, N. (2014). *In the middle, third edition: A lifetime of learning about writing, reading, and adolescents.* Portsmouth, NH: Heinemann.

Bear, D. R., Invernizzi, M.R., Templeton, S.R., & Johnston, F. (2016). *Words their way: Word study for phonics, vocabulary, and spelling instruction* (6th ed.). New York, NY: Pearson.

Beck, I. L., McKeown, M. G., & Kucan, L. (2002). *Bringing words to life.* New York, NY: Guilford.

Bandura, A. (1977). *Social learning theory,* Englewood Cliffs, NJ: Prentice Hall.

Brown, M. (2013). *Tito Puente mambo king rey del mundo.* New York, NY: Harper Collins Publishers.

Browne, A. (2001). *Voices in the Park.* London, UK: DK Publishing.

Calkins, L. M. (1994). *The art of teaching writing.* Portsmouth, NH: Heinemann.

Calkins, L. M. (2014). *Writing pathways: Performance assessments and learning progressions, grades K-8.* Portsmouth, NH: Heinemann.

Clay, M. M. (1991). *Becoming literate: The construction of inner control.* Portsmouth, NH: Heinemann.

Chall, J. S. (1983). *Stage of reading development.* New York, NY: McGraw-Hill.

Clay. M. M., (1985). *The early detection of reading difficulties* (3rd ed.). Portsmouth, NH: Heinemann.

Clay, M. M., (1991a). Introducing a new storybook to young readers. *The Reading Teacher, 45*(4), 264–271.

Clay, M. M., (1991b). *Becoming literate: The construction of inner control.* Auckland, New Zealand: Heinemann.

Collins, J., & Blot, R. K. (2003). *Literacy and literacies: Texts, power, and identity.* New York, NY: Cambridge University Press.

Corson, D. (1997). Awareness of non-standard varieties in the schools. In Van Lier & David Corson (Eds.), *Encyclopedia of language and education* (Vol. 6, pp. 229–240). Norwell, MA: Kluwer Academic Publisher.

Cope, B., & Kalantzis, M. (2002). *Multiliteracies: Literacy learning and design of social futures* (pp. 182–202). New York, NY: Routledge.

Cronin, D. (2011). *Click, clack, moo: Cows that type*. New York, NY: Little Simon: Simon & Schuster.

Cummins, J., & Early, M. (2011). *Identity texts the collaborative creation of power in multilingual schools*. London, England: A Trentham Book.

Cunningham, P. M., Hall, D. P., & Heggie, T. (2001). *Making words, grades 1–3: Multilevel, hands-on phonics and spelling activities*. Greensboro, NC: Good Apple.

DiTerlizzi, T. (2002). *The spider and the fly*. New York, NY: Scholastic.

Duchene, D. A., Smith, C. P,. & Goldfarb, R. A. (2000). Allopurinol induced meningitis. *The Journal of Urology, 164*, 2028.

Ehri, L. C. (1991). Development of the ability to read words. In R. Bass, M. L. Kamil, P. B. Mosenthal, & P. D. Pearson (Eds.), *Handbook of reading research* (Vol. 2, pp. 383–417). New York, NY: Longman.

Fisher, D., & Frey, N. (2014). Addressing CCSS anchor standard 10: Text complexity. *Language Arts, 91*(4), 236–250.

Freire, P. (1970). *Pedagogy of the oppressed*. New York, NY: Herder & Herder.

Freire, P. & Macedo, D. (1987). Literacy: *Reading the word and the world*. New York: NY: Bergin & Garvey Publishers.

Fountas, I. C., & Pinnell, G. S. (1996). *Guided reading: Good first teaching for all children*. Portsmouth, NH: Heinemann.

Fountas, I. C., & Pinnell, G. S. (2012a). Guided reading: The romance and the reality. *The Reading Teacher, 66*(4), 268–284.

Fountas, I., & Pinnell, G. S. (2012b). *Fountas & Pinnell: Prompting guide part 1 for oral reading and early writing*. Portsmouth, NH: Heinemann.

Gansworth, E. (2013). *If I ever get out of here*. New York, NY: Arthur A. Levine Books

Gee, J. P. (2015). *Social linguistics and literacies*. (5th ed.). New York, NY: Routledge.

Goodman, K. S. (1967). Reading: A psycholinguistic guessing game. *Journal of the Reading Specialist, 6*, 126–135.

Gough, P. B., & Tunmer, W. E. (1986). Decoding, reading, and reading disability. *Remedial and Special Education, 7*, 6–10.

Gonzalez, N., Moll, L., & Amanti, C. (2005). Introduction: Theorizing practices. In N. Gonzalez, L. C. Moll, & C. Amanti (Eds.), *Funds of knowledge: Theorizing practices in households, communities, and classrooms* (pp. 1–28). New Jersey: Lawrence Erlbaum.

Goodman, K. S. (1967). Reading: A psycholinguistic guessing game. *Journal of the Reading Specialist, 6*, 126–135.

Graff, H. J. (1987). *The legacies of literacy: Continuities and contradictions in western culture and society*. Indianapolis: Indiana University Press.

Graves, D. H., & Kittle, P. (2005). *Inside writing: How to teach the details of craft*. Portsmouth, NH: Heinemann.

Gusazk, F. J. (1992). *Reading for students with special needs*. Dubuque, IA: Kendall/Hunt Publishing.

Guerra, J. C. (1998). *Close to home: Oral and literate practices in a transnational Mexicano community*. New York, NY: Teachers College Press.

Halliday, M. A. K. (1993). Towards a language-based theory of learning. *Linguistics and Educatio,n 5*(2), 93–116.

Hasbrouck, J., & Tindal, G. (2005). *Oral reading fluency: 90 years of measurement* (Technical Report No. 33). Eugene, OR: Behavioral Research and Teaching, University of Oregon.

Hawkins, M. R. (2013). *Framing languages and literacies: Socially situated views and perspectives* [Kindle version]. Taylor and Francis.

Herobrine Books. (2015). *Diary of a minecraft zombie: Book 1*. San Bernardino, CA: Herobrine Publishing.

Herrera, S. G., Perez, D. R., & K. Escamilla (2014). *Teaching reading to English language learners: Differentiated literacies* (2nd ed.). New York, NY: Pearson.

Joos, M. (1961). *The Five Clocks*. New York, NY: Harcourt, Brace and World.

Juel, C., Griffith, P. L., & Gough, P. B. (1986). Acquisitions of literacy: A longitudinal study of children in first and second grade. *Journal of Educational Psychology, 78*, 243–255.

Kalman, M. (2002). *Fireboat: The heroic adventures of the John J. Harvey*. New York, NY: G. P. Putnam's Sons.

Kress, G. (2002). Multimodality: Why and why now? In Bill Cope & Mary Kalantzis (Eds.), *Multiliteracies: Literacy learning and design of social futures* (pp. 182–202). New York, NY: Routledge.

Kuhn., M. R., Schwanenflugel, P. J., Meisinger, E. B., Levy, B. A., & Rasinski, T. V. (2010). Aligning theory and assessment of reading fluency: Automaticity, prosody, and definitions of fluency. *Reading Research Quarterly, 45*(2), 230–251.

Lapp, D., Flood, J., Brock, C., Fisher, D. (2006). *Teaching reading to every child.* New York, NY: Routledge.

Lave, J., & Wenger, E. (1991). *Situated learning: Legitimate peripheral participation.* Cambridge, England: Cambridge University Press.

Layne, S. L. (2015). In defense of read-aloud: Sustaining best practices. Portland, ME: Stenhouse.

Levine, R. (2000). *Story of the orchestra: Listen while you learn about the instruments, music and composers who wrote the music.* New York, NY: Black Dog and Leventhal Publishers.

Lindfors, J. W. (2008). *Children's language: Connecting reading, writing, and talk.* New York, NY: Teachers College Press.

Marciano, J. (1997). *Civic illiteracy and education: The battle for the hearts and minds of American youth.* New York, NY: Peter Lang Publishing.

McCarrier, A., Pinnell, G. S., & Fountas, I. C. (1999). *Interactive writing: How language & literacy come together.* Portsmouth, NH: Heinemann.

Moll, L., Amanti, C., Neff, D., & Gonzalez, N. (1992). Funds of knowledge for teaching: Using a qualitative approach to connect homes and classrooms. *Theory into practice, 31*(2), 132–141.

Morrow, L.M. (2001). *Literacy development in the early years: Helping children read and write.* (4th ed.) Needham Heights, MA: Allyn & Bacon.

Morrow, L. M., & Gambrell, L. B. (2002). Literature-based instruction in the early years. N. S. B. Neuman & D. K. Dickinson (Eds.), *Handbook of early literacy research* (pp. 348–360). New York, NY: Guilford.

Moss, B., & Hendershot, J. (2002). Exploring sixth graders' selection of nonfiction trade books. *The Reading Teacher, 56*(1), September 2002, pp. 6–17. Published by Wiley on behalf of International Reading Association Stable. Retrieved September 28, 2016 from http://www.jstor.org/stable/20205143

Munson, D. (2000). *Enemy Pie.* San Francisco, CA: Chronicle Books.

National Reading Panel (U.S.), & U.S. National Institute of Child Health and Human Development. (2000). *Report of the National Reading Panel: Teaching children to read: an evidence-based assessment of the scientific research literature on reading and its implications for reading instruction: reports of the subgroups.* Washington, DC: National Institute of Child Health and Human Development, National Institutes of Health.

NBC Learn: *Writers speak to kids.* Retrieved from https://www.nbclearn.com/writers-speak-to-kids.

Neuman, S. B., & Dwyer, J. (2011). Developing vocabulary and conceptual knowledge for low-income preschoolers. A design experiment. *Journal of Literacy Research, 43*(2), 103–129.

Nilsson, N. L. (2008). A critical analysis of eight informal reading inventories. *The Reading Teacher, 61*(7), 526–536.

Ogle, D. M. (1986). K-W-L: A teaching model that develops active reading of expository text. *Reading Teacher 39*, 564–570.

Paris, S. G., & Carpenter, R. D. (2003). FAQs about IRIs. *The Reading Teacher, 56*(6), 578–580.

Price, L. H., Bradley, B. A. (2016). *Revitalizing read alouds: Interactive talk about books with young children, PreK-2.* New York, NY: Teachers College Press.

Rathman, P. (1995). *Officer Buckle and Gloria.* New York: NY: G. P. Putnam's Sons.

Richardson, J. (2009). *The next step in guided reading: Focused assessments and targeted lessons for helping every student become a better reader.* New York, NY: Scholastic.

Rumelhart, D. (1984). Understanding understanding. In J. Flood (Ed.), *Understanding reading comprehension.* Newark, DE: International Reading Association.

Schleppegrell, M. J. (2004). *The language of schooling: A functional linguistics perspective.* Mahwah, NJ: Lawrence Erlbaum Associates.

Schwartz, J. L. (1975). A language experience approach to beginning reading. *Elementary English, 52*(3), 320–324.

Scott, J. A., & Nagy, W. E. (2004). Developing word consciousness. In Eds. J. F. Baumann & E. J. Kame'enui, *Vocabulary instruction: Research to practice* (pp. 201–217). New York, NY: Guilford.

Shulman, L. S. (1986). Those who understand: Knowledge growth in reading. *Educational Researcher, 15*(2), 4–14.

Smith, F. (1971). *Understanding reading: A psycholinguistic analysis of reading and learning to read.* New York, NY: Holt, Rinehart & Winston.

Smith, N. B. (2002/1934). *American reading instruction.* Newark, DE: International Reading Association.

Snow, C. E., Burns, M. S. & Griffith, P. (1998). *Preventing reading difficulties in young children.* Washington, DC: National Academy Press.

Street, B. (2013). Literacy in theory and practice: Challenges and debates over 50 years. *Theory into practice, 52*(1), 52–62.

Swartz, S. L., Shook, R. E., & Klein, A. F. (2002). *Shared reading: Reading with children.* Parsippany, NJ: Dominie Press.

Taylor, D. (1983). *Family literacy.* Exeter, NH: Heinemann Educational Books.

Tompkins, G. E. (2013). *50 literacy strategies: Step by step* (4th ed.). New York, NY: Pearson.

Tracey, D. H., & Morrow, L. M. (2012). *Lenses on reading: An introduction to theories and models.* New York, NY: Guilford Press.

Turner, J. C. (1995). The influence of classroom contexts on young children's motivation for literacy. *Reading Research Quarterly, 30*(3), 410–441. doi:10.2307/747624

Vygotsky, L. S. (1978). *Mind in society: The development of higher psychological processes.* Cambridge, MA: MIT Press.

Webster, J. J., & Halliday, M. A. K. (2016). *Aspects of language and learning* [Kindle version]. Springer Berlin Heidelberg.

Williams-Garcia, R. (2013). *P.S. be eleven.* New York, NY: Harper Collins Publishers.

Williams, C., Phillips-Birdsong, C., Hufnagel, K., Hungler, D., & Lundstrom, R. P. (2009). Word study instruction in the K-2 classroom. *The Reading Teacher, 6*(7), 570–578.

Winter, J. (2008). *Roberto Clemente: Pride of the Pittsburgh Pirates.* New York, NY: Atheneum Books.

Wood, A., & Wood, D. (2009). *The Napping House.* New York, NY: HMH Books for Young Readers.

Woods, M. L. & Moe, A. J. (2011). Analytical reading inventory: Comprehensive standards-based assessment for all students including gifted and remedial (9th ed.). New York, NY: Pearson.

Zinshteyn, M. (2014). American students who struggle with English outnumber kids born abroad. *The Atlantic* (December 24, 2014). Retrieved July 1, 2016 from http://www.theatlantic.com/education/archive/2014/12/american-students-who-struggle-with-english-outnumber-kids-born-abroad/384004/

APPENDICES

APPENDICES FOR CHAPTER 2

Appendix 2.1

K-W-L

Know	Want to Learn	Learned

Appendix 2.2

Getting to Know Your Student—Reflection Guide

Guiding Questions	Reflective Thoughts
What did you learn about your student's language, literacy background, and practices?	
What information surprised you or did you find interesting?	
How will you begin to use this information to guide your lesson development?	
What did you learn about your own literacy background?	
Other thoughts or ideas? Any further questions you might have for your student?	

APPENDICES FOR CHAPTER 6

Appendix 6.1

Modeled Reading Log

Title of Book	Book Level	Genre	Accuracy Rate	Fluency	Comprehension	Assessment

Key:

Book Level: As indicated by publisher
Genre: Narrative or expository
Accuracy Rate: Percentage of words read correctly
Fluency: Quantitative (WPM) or qualitative (- or +)
Comprehension: Retelling (- or +)
Assessment: Overall level of book including all elements (independent, instructional, frustrational)

APPENDICES FOR CHAPTER 7

Appendix 7.1

Modeled Reading Log

Title of Book	Book Level	Genre	Accuracy Rate	Fluency	Comprehension	Assessment

Key:

Book Level: As indicated by publisher
Genre: Narrative or expository
Accuracy Rate: Percentage of words read correctly
Fluency: Quantitative (WPM) or qualitative (- or +)
Comprehension: Retelling (- or +)
Assessment: Overall level of book including all elements (independent, instructional, frustrational)

APPENDICES FOR CHAPTER 8

Appendix 8.1

Writing Log

Date	Title	Genre			Process					Assessment Notes
		Narrative	Informational	Opinion	Prewriting	Drafting	Revising	Editing	Publishing	

GLOSSARY

Accuracy: Accuracy is the number of words read correctly.

Author's Chair: In author's chair, students have the opportunity to sit in front of their peers and share all or a portion of their work.

Confidentiality: Maintaining confidentiality means not openly discussing your student's personal and family information with others. In addition, we do not share videos or photos of the student online without written permission.

Comprehension: Comprehension is making meaning from text.

Content Knowledge: Content knowledge refers to the foundational knowledge of the field or discipline taught (Shulman, 1986).

Cueing Systems: Meaning/semantics refers to how readers use the meaning of the text as they read.

Decoding/visual/graphophonic refers to how readers use letters/word/parts as they read. It can also refer to how readers use illustrations/graphics as they read.

Grammar/syntax refers to how readers use their knowledge of language structures as they read.

Curricular Materials: Curricular materials include any type of programs or materials used during instruction.

Developmental Levels: Developmental reading levels are the predictable stages of reading that young readers go through as they learn to read.

Developmental Level in Relation to the Writer: Young writers' developmental levels are based on their ability to draft their ideas fluently, knowledge of spelling, use of their oral language vocabulary, the complexity of their sentence structure, and their ability to express ideas in sequence.

Drafting:	Drafting is the stage of writing in which writers record their ideas quickly and fluently.
Editing:	Editing includes checking the writing for spelling, punctuation, and grammar.
English Learner:	An English learner (EL) is a student whose first or home language is a language other than English and who most often relies on that language to successfully communicate.
Fluency:	Fluency is reading quickly with expression and understanding.
Funds of Knowledge:	Funds of knowledge are the types of conventional and nonconventional literacies students have access to in their household and community. It is the knowledge students bring with them to the instructional setting.
Genres:	Genre means type or kind. In children's literature genre refers to the specific type of text selected, such as picture book, realistic fiction, historical fiction, fantasy, poetry, traditional literature, or nonfiction.
Guided Reading:	Guided reading requires the use of instructional level texts during lessons to help readers improve. These are texts that are read with at least 90% accuracy and with good understanding.
Independent Reading Level:	The student's independent reading level is a text the student can easily read on his or her own without much support.
Identity Texts:	Identity texts are written works created by students about themselves.
Instructional Level:	Guided reading requires the use of instructional level texts during lessons to help readers improve. These are texts that are read with at least 90% accuracy and with good understanding.
Interactive Read Aloud:	An interactive read aloud involves active student participation and strategic instruction.
Interactive/ Shared Writing:	Interactive/shared writing means sharing the writing task with students to assist them with unknown words or difficult aspects of texts.
Language Registers:	Language registers are the various types of styles used depending on context and audience.
LEA:	LEA allows students to dictate their writing ideas as you write for them. It provides a model of writing and helps students understand the process of writing and spelling as they observe you writing.
Lexile System:	The Lexile system can be used to find a book leveled at your student's approximate reading level.
Literacy:	Literacy is a broad term that moves beyond simple reading and writing. Literacy includes in-depth knowledge about a topic and the ability to listen, speak, read, and write.
Multimodal Literacy:	Multimodal literacy recognizes the various types of texts and modes we use today beyond just books.

Mentor Text:	Mentor texts are usually written (but can also be multimodal) texts students can use as a model for their writing.
Nonstandard Varieties of English:	Nonstandard English includes types of English vocabulary and grammar that deviates from what is considered to be the standard practice of spoken and written English used in academic arenas.
Pedagogical Content Knowledge:	Pedagogical content knowledge refers to the knowledge of various ways to break down the content to make it understandable to students (Shulman, 1986).
Phonemic Awareness:	Phonemic awareness is the ability to hear and segment sounds in words orally.
Phonics:	Phonics is understanding the relationship between letters and sounds.
Prewriting:	Prewriting involves discussing the topic with your student, showing examples, and taking notes or drawing pictures.
Prompting:	Prompting is what reading teachers do as students read to assist them with unknown words or difficult aspects of texts.
Publishing:	Publishing a student's writing is the final stage of the writing process. Publication involves finding a final piece of writing to revise, edit, polish and present.
Read aloud:	A read aloud is an excellent opportunity to model reading aloud with expression and intonation to your student
Revising:	Revising drafts is focused on adding ideas, making changes, organizing ideas, and elaborating on ideas.
Text Level in Relation to Specific Criteria:	Text level is measured by the type of vocabulary, the frequency of specific words, the complexity of the sentence structure, and the content or genre.
Text Level in Relation to the Reader:	The level of difficulty of a text is shaped by the content as it relates to the reader's knowledge, the vocabulary as it relates to the reader's word knowledge, the complexity of the sentence structure, and the reader's motivation to read it.
Think Aloud:	Thinking aloud involves talking about all of the aspects of writing, including ideas, word choice, sentence structure, and spelling. It allows students to hear how authors think as they write.
Vocabulary:	Vocabulary is understanding word meanings.
Writing Informational Texts:	Informational texts are designed to be informative and factual, and are structured to provide detailed information about specific topics.
Writing Level in Relation to Specific Genre:	There are many types of writing. We are relying on personal narratives, report/research writing, and opinion/argument writing.
Writing Opinion Texts:	Opinion writing requires taking a particular stance and trying to persuade others to agree with you.